TAMING THE FAMILY
ZOO

TAMING THE FAMILY ZOO

Maximizing Harmony and Minimizing Family Stress

JIM AND SUZETTE BRAWNER

NAVPRESS●

BRINGING TRUTH TO LIFE

NavPress Publishing Group

P.O. Box 35001, Colorado Springs, Colorado 80935

The Navigators is an international Christian organization. Our mission is to reach, disciple, and equip people to know Christ and to make Him known through successive generations. We envision multitudes of diverse people in the United States and every other nation who have a passionate love for Christ, live a lifestyle of sharing Christ's love, and multiply spiritual laborers among those without Christ.

NavPress is the publishing ministry of The Navigators. NavPress publications help believers learn biblical truth and apply what they learn to their lives and ministries. Our mission is to stimulate spiritual formation among our readers.

Library of Congress Catalog Card Number: 98-9717
ISBN 1-57683-058-6

Cover illustration: by Cyd Moore/Irmeli Holmberg

Some of the anecdotal illustrations in this book are true to life and are included with the permission of the persons involved. All other illustrations are composites of real situations, and any resemblance to people living or dead is coincidental. Certain names and other details pertaining to the case studies presented in this book have been changed to protect the privacy of the individuals involved.

The following have been used by permission: "Too Cold at Home," by Bobby L. Harden; "Heroes," by Paul Overstreet and Claire Cloninger; "She Keeps the Home Fires Burning," by Mike Reid, Don Pfrimmer, and Dennis Morgan.

Unless otherwise identified, all Scripture quotations in this publication are taken from the *HOLY BIBLE: NEW INTERNATIONAL VERSION* ® (NIV®). Copyright © 1973, 1978, 1984 by International Bible Society. Used by permission of Zondervan Publishing House. All rights reserved; and the *New American Standard Bible* (NASB), ©The Lockerman Foundation 1960, 1962, 1963, 1968, 1971, 1972, 1973, 1975, 1977.

Brawner, Jim.
   Taming the family zoo : maximizing harmony and minimizing family stress / Jim and Suzette Brawner.
      p.   cm.
   ISBN 1-57683-058-6 (pbk.)
   1. Parenting. 2. Child rearing. 3. Parent and child. 4. Parenting—Religious aspects. I. Brawner, Suzette, 1951– . II. Title.
HQ755.8.B728   1998
649'.1—dc21   98-9717
                                                                                  CIP

Printed in the United States of America

1 2 3 4 5 6 7 8 9 10 11 12 13 14 15 / 03 02 01 00 99 98

Published in association with the literary agency of
Wolgemuth & Hyatt, Inc.,
Brentwood, Tennessee

To our parents
Mr. and Mrs. O. R. Brawner
and
Dr. and Mrs. Fred R. Bollen,
who have a combined 106 years of marriage.
That is a commitment matched by few couples today.

Acknowledgments

We would like to express our deepest thanks to the following people:

To our children—Jason, Travis, and Jill, and Jason's wife, Alison. Thank you for your unconditional love as we still learn how to parent.

To (Jim's) brothers, Jerry and Joe Brawner, and to my sister, Janet Freeman, who have weathered the storms and enjoyed the sunshine in life with me.

And to my (Suzette's) brother, Russ Bollen—thanks for being my friend. I love you.

To Gary Smalley and John Trent, the two best coaches we have ever had. Their encouragement and direction kept this dream alive.

To Spike and Darnell White, who over the past twenty-five years have been finishing the parenting job that our parents began.

And finally to Traci Mullins, our editor, who gave us enough encouragement and support to get us over writer's block and help us reach our ultimate goal.

Contents

foreword

Every time I read a parenting book, I secretly wish I could peek in on the author's family to see if they are really living what they write about. I've been able to do that with the Brawner family for over twenty years. I have watched them in every possible family situation. We've been close friends for such a long time that I feel I'm part of their family.

When Jim and Suzette Brawner give advice on parenting, we can take it right to the bank and be assured of receiving high interest on our investment! They have already lived it, and the proof is in their children's lives and accomplishments. Jason, now twenty-three, a thirteen-time All-American collegiate swimmer, is a graphic designer living in Branson, Missouri, with his wife, Alison, who is a kindergarten teacher. Travis, twenty-one, is a premed student at Southwest Missouri State University where he is an All-American football player. Jill, seventeen, a beautiful young lady, is very involved at Branson High School where she is on the varsity volleyball and track teams. All three children are honoring, loving individuals any parent would be extremely proud of.

In this book you'll learn how to motivate your children to greatly honor others so they can become productive citizens and a real encouragement to their community. You'll see what Jim and Suzette have done to show appreciation for each of their children as unique individuals, to understand their feelings and needs, to laugh with them, and to gain encouragement and wisdom for the tough times.

Something I appreciate about Jim and Suzette is that they never intended to write a book about parenting. It happened because several of their friends, including Norma and me, kept pushing them until they finally gave in to the difficult and sometimes grueling work. They have succeeded marvelously as authors and especially as parents. I count it an honor to be called their friend.

GARY SMALLEY

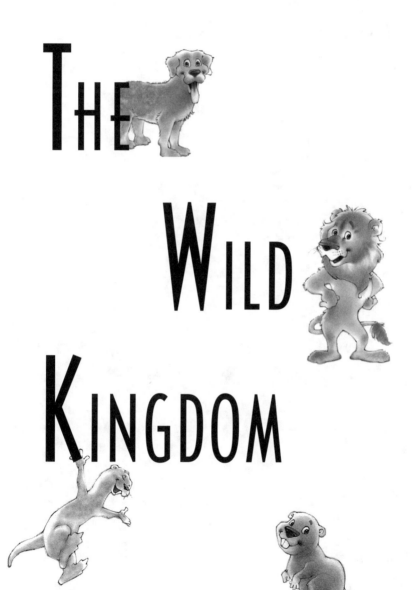

PART ONE

THE WILD KINGDOM

CHAPTER ONE
It's a Jungle Out There

LET US TAKE YOU BACK SEVERAL YEARS TO A TYPICAL EARLY evening scene in the Brawner household. The clock had just struck 5 P.M.—feeding time at the Brawner Zoo. Suzette and I herded our three offspring into the minivan and ventured forth into the flashing lights of Branson's fast-food jungle.

As we made our way down Country Music Boulevard in Branson, Missouri—home to every burger, chicken, pizza, and ice cream franchise in the known universe—the rumbling of stomachs moved to the vocal chords.

Travis knew exactly what he wanted. "Wendy's is where we're going!" he roared. It's a Dave's Deluxe burger or nothing for our middle child.

Suzette—practical by nature—approaches a fast-food safari armed with a fistful of coupons. "Wendy's has a buy-one-get-one-free sale, so let's be thrifty and go there," she urged.

Jill and I scanned the neon jungle of over eighty music shows and twice that many restaurants for a place packed with people.

"Let's just drive down the road and wherever the action is, let's go there!" Jill contributed. If the eating spot had lots of kids, a slide, a roomful of plastic balls to jump into, or a "fun meal," that settled it for our daughter.

Jason waited to hear what other family members wanted.

"Where would you like to eat, Jason?" was generally answered with, "Whatever makes everyone else happy, I'm willing to go along."

Fortunately the Wendy's parking lot was packed because of the buy-one-get-one-free offer on Dave's Deluxes, so all was well with the entire Brawner clan—at least momentarily. Through the years, as our three kids were growing up, Suzette and I have seen what could have seemed like total chaos turn into a stimulating exercise in patience, reinforcing the bond between parent and child. Raising children is hard, tedious, exhausting work. However, the benefits outweigh any alternatives a zoo keeper might choose to exercise.

Our family structure has changed significantly since that long-ago ride down the strip for dinner. Jason, a college graduate and a freelance graphic designer, is married and living in our hometown. We've watched this please-at-all-cost person grow up into a loving man who has developed the ability to stand his ground. Alison, his wife, is just the balance he needed.

Travis, our model strong-willed child, is a junior in college pursuing a biology degree with plans for medical school. He has acquired a more balanced approach to life through some painful lessons that have forced him to learn patience. If we had not learned to honor, discipline, understand, and value his uniqueness, Travis could easily have ended up on a path of destruction. He is currently a 4.0 student and is handling all the kicking for his college football team.

Our third child was literally our bouncing baby girl. Jill, now a junior in high school, has had to learn time management and organizational skills. As anyone can attest, this is quite a challenge for someone with a bent toward the sociability of a sea otter. By understanding her personality, we were able to predict her challenges at an early age. We worked with her to avoid potentially disastrous situations and encourage balance.

Our family—and we'd be willing to guess yours, too—features a menagerie of different personality types. Through the years our home has reverberated with the sights and sounds of a robust wild kingdom. But that doesn't mean we had to take on a "survival of the fittest" mentality—and neither do you. The goal of parenting is not to make carbon copies of ourselves, but to produce happy, healthy originals.

In this book we'll share with you the parenting principles we began practicing years ago and still use successfully today. Back in 1990, Gary Smalley and Dr. John Trent, authors of *The Two Sides of Love*, encouraged us to adapt the concepts they teach about basic personality types and use them to help parents improve their parenting skills. We discovered that when family members understand their uniqueness and appreciate each other's basic differences, they can avoid the major problems that result if each person is not understood and cared for as a unique individual.

The number-one teenage complaint and alleged cause of suicide among kids aged thirteen to eighteen is weak relationships at home. We'll help you understand how these teens and children of all ages view life, and how you can adapt your parenting style to those differences. You'll learn key principles of communication—both verbal and nonverbal—and discover how your actions affect your kids for better or worse. You'll find out how to motivate your children in honest and effective ways—maximizing family harmony and minimizing family stress and friction.

WORRISOME TRENDS IN THE WILD KINGDOM

Before we get into how better to understand each other, we need to take a step back and look at the social landscape. How are families in America faring today? And, more important, how is society affecting your particular family?

Unfortunately, all is not well in American familyland. Many times we indulge in a little self-delusion and either ignore or minimize the bad things that are happening in families today, but that doesn't solve the problems. We need to look bravely at what the environment around us is like so we can better combat the destructive forces that can work their way into our homes.

My (Jim's) personal crusade began one Saturday morning several years ago as I sat in my favorite restaurant reading the paper. On the front page was an article about Jan, a student from the high school where I coached and taught. Jan was a bright, attractive, "A" student in my tenth-grade health class. She had few friends. A loner by choice, I thought.

Just twenty-four hours earlier I had stood in my first-hour class as the usual "Friday frenzy" filled the classroom with excitement about the weekend ahead. "Today, we'll review the last test," I announced. "According to the scores it looks like we need to go over the section on social pressure and how it affects us individually." Jan had aced the test, as usual—but little did I know the topic was not just an academic exercise for her. Suddenly she burst into tears, bolted from her chair, and dashed from the classroom. As the students sat in stunned silence, my eyes focused on Leanne, one of Jan's few friends.

"Leanne, why don't you check on Jan?" The students watched silently as Leanne left.

"Okay, class," I continued, trying to pull the students' focus back to the test results. "Let's turn in our books to page seventy-eight." Everyone had a difficult time keeping his or her attention on the test review after Jan's unexplained outburst.

Moments before the bell sounded, Jan and Leanne finally returned to the classroom. Jan's red eyes and smeared mascara testified that something was very wrong. I asked Jan and Leanne to remain after the bell rang.

"Jan," I began, "is there some way I can help?"

She stared at the floor as she wiped away more tears.

"It's just some trouble at home. I'll be okay."

"Would you like to talk about it?"

"No. I'll be okay, Mr. Brawner." She got up quickly and hurried to her next class.

That was the last time I ever talked with Jan.

The next day in the restaurant I stared in disbelief at the newspaper headline: "Teen in Critical Condition Following Suicide Attempt." Jan had taken her father's .38 revolver, shoved the barrel into her mouth, and pulled the trigger. After a twelve-hour medical effort to save her life, the fifteen-year-old girl died, her life cruelly and irretrievably snuffed out. I was devastated, as were Jan's classmates.

When school resumed on Monday, the loss of a classmate echoed down subdued halls and screamed out from the empty chair in each class period. I found it practically impossible to concentrate when my eyes fell on Jan's chair. I wanted to cry.

I learned from Leanne that Jan's parents had filed for divorce, and the final papers had been signed on the Friday Jan fled from my classroom. I also learned that although Jan had not been physically abused, she had been verbally abused. Cuts and bruises heal, but cruel words can shred children like bullets.

I've asked myself a thousand times, *How could I have discovered Jan's deep emotional needs early enough to intervene? What could I have done to help her parents affirm her? How can I keep other Jans from ending their lives? How can I help other parents see how powerful—and deadly—unkind words can be?*

GROPING TOWARD INTIMACY

Unfortunately, healthy families are rapidly becoming an endangered species. At the root of many families' troubles lies a problem we call *disconnectedness*. Moms and dads, sons and daughters are reaching in the dark, groping to communicate and truly understand each other. They want to find an intimate, warm connection with each other, but often they lack the tools.

This situation is described well in the song, "Too Cold at Home." The singer is sitting in a tavern on a hot summer's day, drowning his sorrows in a cold beer. He's not motivated to go home to his wife. As he puts it:

"It's too hot to fish,
too hot for golf,
and too cold at home."[1]

Too many families today are merely collections of isolated individuals. They're estranged from each other, and they desperately need to connect.

MORAL MEGATRENDS

The disintegration of the American family did not start yesterday; it's been gathering steam over the past few decades. In 1989, Ronald Levant, a family researcher at Boston University, described five forces he believes contributed to the development of the contemporary family's situation[2]: (1) new family planning technologies and practices (giving couples the power to decide if and when to have children); (2) explosion of the divorce rate (with the inception of no-fault divorce); (3) child custody innovations (with blended families and single-parent families commonplace and six out of ten children born in the nineties living in a single-parent home before they are eighteen years old[3]); (4) increase in employment of women; and (5) decrease in the standard of living (for example, salaries not keeping up with housing prices).

In our opinion, Dr. Levant put his finger on several real

forces that have shaped American families through the years. What he failed to take into account, however, is a moral megatrend during the fifties and sixties that gave us a humanistic morality, the sexual revolution, and a distrust—if not disrespect—for all authority figures.

Judeo-Christian values had been generally accepted by society at large for most of the past two millennia. Lifelong monogamous relationships between husband and wife, although not practiced by all, were at least the cultural ideal. Parents, police officers, and government officials were generally respected as servants who looked out for our best interests. But all of that changed during the '50s and '60s. And these mega-shifts were reflected in TV families.

During the '50s, Beaver Cleaver never came home to an empty house after school. Latchkey kids were unheard of then. And grass was something he whined about having to mow on Saturday morning. Ward, the wise and warm patriarch of the Cleaver family, apparently made enough money so June didn't have to work outside the home. Instead she could wear designer dresses and pearls as she made dinner—from scratch. Ward's main at-home role was to provide a two-minute moral lesson that neatly resolved any trouble that the Beaver, brother Wally, and "the guys" got into.

In the late '60s and early '70s a shift in the family structure was evident with the advent of "The Brady Bunch." When widowed mom Carol married widowed, handsome architect, Bob, they combined their three precious blond girls and three all-American boys into the ideal blended family. They had a live-in housekeeper and life was still a bit "Cleaverish," but real blended family issues were addressed. "The Courtship of Eddie's Father" and "The Partridge Family" also came onto the scene, exploring the single-parent world and some of its inherent challenges.

In the '80s and '90s, the Keatons of "Family Ties" and the Huxtables of "The Cosby Show" reflected some of the realities of dual-income families and the changes we were experiencing as a society as a whole. The long-running sitcoms "Married . . . With Children" and "Roseanne" were enough to depress the most encouraged family advocates. For example, Roseanne Conner dealt with sibling rivalry by shouting at her two daughters, "All right, you two, fight to the death!"

And finally, we have the modern thermonuclear family, "The Simpsons." Compared to Bart Simpson, the Conner kids seem almost respectful and obedient. With one of Bart's favorite phrases being "Eat my shorts," he's no Beaver Cleaver.

Some family experts explain the popularity of these shows as a reaction to the saccharine-sweet situation comedies of the '50s and '60s. Fathers are not always right. Mothers do not vacuum in designer dresses. Not all children are candidates for Eagle Scouts or are as polite as the Beav.

True. But neither are all fathers incompetent, insensitive, insulting losers with an IQ only slightly higher than their belt size. Not all mothers have lousy sex lives, lousy jobs, lousy hairstyles, and even lousier kids. And not all kids are as rude as Bart.

A REASON TO HOPE

Not long ago, I (Suzette) was talking to my sister-in-law, Rayanna. She called me, discouraged, after listening to a radio broadcast on parenting. "I am so tired of hearing about what all we, as parents, have done wrong," she said. "I wanted to call in to the show and say, 'I've worked hard at the job of parenting. Please tell me that I've done something right.' I think I've done a darn good job!" Rayanna and Jerry are raising three daughters, and she's right: they *are* doing a good job!

As parents, we all need plenty of encouragement and positive input. If your family, like ours, falls somewhere between the Cleavers and the Conners, then you need not despair. The practical, field-tested principles we describe in the pages that follow have worked in our family and many other families—and they can in yours. Here you'll learn how better to understand yourself and those unique and bewildering creatures called children. We'll share some ideas on motivating your children based on their personality makeup. You'll discover how to instill your beliefs and values into your kids and increase your effectiveness as a parent. Most important, you'll find out how to keep your family off the endangered species list.

In the next chapter we'll give you an overview of the principles we've discovered that can help you increase the odds of your home becoming a peaceful game preserve.

THINKING IT OVER

1. When your family heads out to the fast-food jungle, what transpires in your car?
2. What are some unique attractions or activities in your area that are conducive to family fun? Of these, which ones do the various family members favor? Why? Do you see a pattern emerging with regard to their preferences?
3. In what specific ways do you think the changes in society since the "Leave It to Beaver" era are affecting your family today?
4. What family do you know that seems to "have it all together"? Why do you think they have experienced such success?

Notes

1. Bobby L. Harden, "Too Cold at Home." Copyright ©1990 by EMI April Music, Inc. and K-Mark Music. All rights controlled and administered by EMI April Music, Inc. All rights reserved. International copyright secured. Used by permission.
2. "When Kids Go Down the Tubes: Eight Stories You Won't See on Sitcoms," *People*, March 25, 1991, p. 38-39.
3. George Barna, *The Frog in the Kettle* (Ventura, Calif.: Regal, 1990), p. 66.

CHAPTER TWO

Identifying the Uniqueness of Your Own Critters

YEARS AGO ON A TRIP TO THE ZOO IN LITTLE ROCK, ARKANSAS, we saw once again what unique "animals" make up the Brawner menagerie.

As usual, lionhearted Travis had the entire day planned. "First we're gonna see the lions and the tigers, and then we've gotta see the poisonous snake exhibit. That's my favorite!" Simply seeing some animals during a nice day at the zoo was not his goal—seeing *all* the animals was. And he was going to direct our movements as well.

By contrast, Jill and Jim viewed the day as a chance to take in as many exhibits as possible. The fun-loving part of them wanted to be sure to see the monkeys and gorillas.

Jason, who's usually the "whatever makes everyone happy" member of our family, preferred to spend the whole day at the petting pavilion. He would rather make friends with just a few animals than see five hundred of them in one afternoon.

I (Suzette) always see a trip to the zoo—or anywhere else—as a time to be with the family. I majored on the relational aspects of our outing.

As you can see, there is a wide variety of personalities in family zoos. And it's important to allow each individual the freedom to roam beyond his or her preconceived category.

ZOOS: THEN AND NOW

Zoos once consisted of concrete buildings with long hallways lined with cages sided with heavy steel bars. Each exhibit was clearly pigeonholed as to its kingdom, phylum, class, order, family, genus, and species.

There was the wild cat building where lions, tigers, and cheetahs paced back and forth on the cement floor waiting for feeding time. In the primate house, monkeys, chimps, and gorillas climbed bars, swung on tire swings, and snatched up peanuts in their steel and concrete enclosures.

In modern zoos, however, there are few pigeonholes. Animals roam in natural environments. Chimps scamper among imported trees, rocks, and exotic grasses that imitate their native environment. Lions live together in prides and prowl acres of African grasses as visitors ride through their domain in their own cars or safari jeeps on rails.

Franklin Park Zoo in Boston has even solved the problem of northern winters. The revamped zoo features a three-acre domed building with a seventy-five-foot ceiling. Inside the temperature controlled building, twenty-five species of birds and snakes as well as gorillas, leopards, mandrills, and bongos feel at home among the waterfalls, rocks, cliffs, and foliage.

The family zoo has undergone some dramatic changes in the past thirty years as well. Some trends, as we saw in the previous chapter, haven't been positive. But one positive change is the realization that all children do not fit neatly into one category.

As you have noticed, Jill, Jason, and Travis have three different types of personalities. It's amazing that the same parents in the same environment can produce such variety.

YOUR MENAGERIE

About four hundred years before Christ, Hippocrates, a Greek physician, divided the human race into four temperaments based on a person's balance of four "humors," or body fluids: choleric (choler), melancholy (black bile), phlegmatic (phlegm), and sanguine (blood).

These categories are no longer taken seriously by modern medicine, but the Hippocrates hypothesis did provide some important insights. First, our body's health does affect our outlook on life. For example, doctors are discovering that some kinds of depression result from a biochemical deficiency in the nervous system that can be treated with prescription drugs. Second, Hippocrates was correct that certain types of people seem to approach life in a similar manner.

Psychologists today cannot agree on how many types of critters roam this planet. In fact, they can't even agree on how generally to classify these very different people. For our purposes we're going to define personality as *an individual's characteristic pattern of behavior and thought*. Each person has a unique set of character traits. That doesn't mean that he or she will always act in character, but there is an overall, general pattern for most people's behavior and thought. Personality, then, is not *who* we are, but *how* we act and react in most situations.

Family harmony—and strife—occurs when very different kinds of personalities begin rubbing against each other. Sparks can fly, as any parent knows. Given the wonderful variety of children in our families, it would be ludicrous to raise them all the same way. Yet that's what many parents try to do.

Before we begin talking about various types of personalities, we strongly suggest that you take time right now to have each member of your family fill out one of the following surveys.[1] You may want to photocopy more surveys so there are enough for all the members of your family.

After you have filled in the adult or child survey, plot the results on the graph. Take the number of words or sentences you circled and make a bar chart in each category.

For example, if you circled three words for list L, make a dot on the L scale three points high (see left-hand values). Then connect the dots between the four scales to make a graph. We'll discuss the meaning of the graph later on.

As we describe various personality types, keep in mind that no type is right or wrong, better or worse. They're just different. The categories simply describe the characteristic ways we think and respond to situations. Also, be aware that no one is 100 percent purebred. We are all various mixes of personality types.

THE FOUR PERSONALITY TYPES

Let's preview the four types of personalities we'll be discussing in this book: the Lion, the Otter, the Golden Retriever, and the Beaver. (Before you read this material, I urge you again to take the personality test first. If you don't, your test results may be influenced by the information below.)

To briefly illustrate the four personality types, consider this story. If all four personality types fell off the Empire State Building, they would all experience the same event. But because of their unique personalities, they would have four unique reactions.

The Lion would say, "We're all as good as dead!" Lions want to get to the bottom line—literally in this case!

The Beaver would calculate, "We'll all be dead in thirty seconds." Beavers like precision and planning.

The Golden Retriever wouldn't say anything but would be looking for a paw to hold. To Retrievers togetherness and relationships are more important than outcomes.

And the Otter would observe, "So far, so good!" Otters are eternal optimists.

The animal-based system we use is not the only personality typing system around. Some of the more popular and

Personality Survey for Adults

Choose those words or phrases that describe you.

List L
Assertive
Competitive
Decisive
Adventurous
Goal-driven

List O
Fun-loving
Motivator
Avoids details
Optimistic
Enjoys change

List R
Loyal
Deep relationships
Avoids conflict
Adaptable
Dislikes change

List B
Orderly
Predictable
Precise, factual
Discerning, analytical
Persistent

Total the number of words circled in each list:

L:_____ O:_____ R:_____ B:_____

Personality Survey for Children

Choose the sentences that are most like you.

List L
I like being the leader.
I say what I think.
I don't like a lot of rules.
I hate to lose games.
I'm not often scared.

List O
I'm funny and playful.
Others like my ideas.
My room is often messy.
I know lots of people.
I like to talk to people.

List R
I have a few close friends.
I'm loyal to my friends.
I want to please others.
I'm kind to others.
I don't like big changes.

List B
I like to do things right.
My room is often neat.
I often hide my feelings.
I'm not good enough.
I do well at school.

Write below the number of sentences you circled in each list:

L:_____ O:_____ R:_____ B:_____

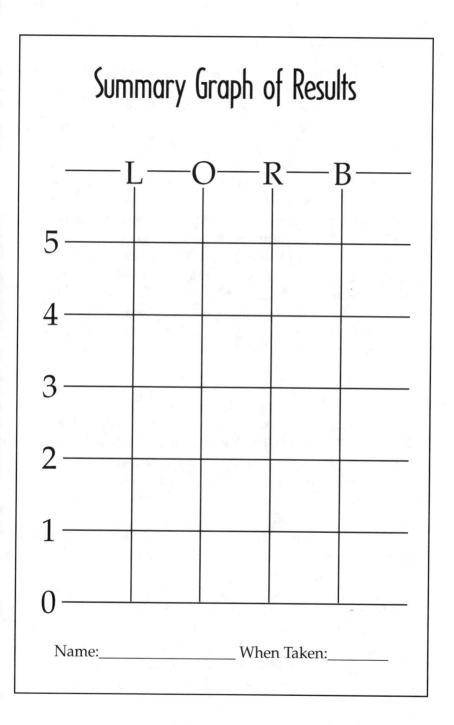

widely used ones are the Myers-Briggs Type Indicator, the Taylor-Johnson Temperament Analysis, the Minnesota Multiphasic Personality Inventory (MMPI), and Birth Order concepts. (See the Appendix for a brief discussion of these systems.)

So there are several valid ways of looking at and organizing our behavior. But I've found the animal-based system we describe to be the best, especially in terms of reliability, comprehensiveness, and ease of understanding. It was developed by Gary Smalley and Dr. John Trent, based partially on the Personal Profile System (DiSC by Performax).[2] Gary and John examined that test, plus thirty others, in an attempt to formulate a user-friendly yet highly reliable personality assessment tool. They have done an outstanding job in developing the tool, and I am grateful to them for their input.

INTERPRETING YOUR RESULTS

Now let's interpret the survey you and your family members filled out. Your test will probably have words circled in each of the categories. Most who take this personality test find that they score high in one or two categories and low in one or two categories. And in most cases there is one type that is dominant over the others.

The most important chart is the bar chart where you plotted the strength of each trait. It graphically reveals the fact that none of us is purely any one type—we're all blends of the four traits. Nevertheless, you'll probably have one or two scales that are higher than the others. The ideal is to have a healthy balance of all four animal traits.

As you look over your results, keep in mind that our goal is not neatly to classify—as the older zoos did—but to gain a general understanding of ourselves and the other personalities that make up our unique family zoo. The principles in this book will help you understand how you relate to others and how others relate to you. And by knowing this, you'll be better able to understand your family and motivate your children.

Now let's look at each of the four personality types in a bit more detail.

L is for Lion

As we picture the king of the jungle in our minds, we see one who boldly takes charge and is assertive and determined. Those with Lion personalities are goal-driven and enjoy difficult challenges. They climb Mount Everest "because it's there" and are always looking for a goal to achieve. If the neighborhood children are playing school, the Lion is the principal. If the children are playing backyard baseball, he appoints himself the captain.

Our second-born, Travis, is the Lion of our family. You can usually spot a strong Lion without a personality test. He or she has an opinion on every subject. (Remember Travis's reactions as we searched for a fast-food restaurant on Country Music Boulevard? He made clear that it was Wendy's or nowhere.)

We parents are also a combination of personality types. So as we discuss the various animals, be aware that your personality mix also plays a large role in the makeup of your menagerie. For instance, if both child and parent are Lions, there is a tendency to come at each other with fangs bared. In fact, Lions actually gain energy from confrontations—whereas Golden Retrievers run for cover.

We'll talk more specifically about understanding and motivating Lions—and the other personality types—in later chapters. We'll cover in depth what motivates and discourages this type, along with their strengths and weaknesses.

O is for Otter

Those who score high in the O category are extremely verbal and social. The Otter personality, like its furry counterpart, is fun-loving, energetic, and impulsive. They're great talkers and motivators but hate details and are often shortsighted.

Our third-born, Jill, and her dad are Otters. (Jim is about half Otter and half Golden Retriever.) You can easily recognize an Otter's room. The bed—if made at all—is just thrown together. The floor is cluttered with half-finished puzzles, partially colored pictures, and two-thirds of a LEGO® project. Otters love starting things but often get distracted by new opportunities before the original project is completed.

One important—and possibly lifesaving—bit of advice: Never, never, never open an Otter's closet. Jill's idea of cleaning her room is to stuff everything into her closet. You open her closet door at your own risk!

A parent who is predominantly Otter will have a good time with his or her children but will run into problems if that trait is allowed to run wild. We'll discuss this more fully in chapter 4.

R is for Retriever

Golden Retrievers are the most loyal personality type. They're tolerant, sympathetic, and easygoing. They're "man's best friend" because they're motivated by relationships and the approval of others. However, they're extremely eager to please, so decision making is difficult because they don't want to offend anyone. Retrievers' walls are usually covered with pictures of their friends and posters of their heroes. Retrievers are almost the purest form of "people people."

Unless they have some Lion blood, Retrievers can be pushovers as parents. They tend to cave in to children's demands because they want so badly to keep everyone happy.

Our firstborn, Jason, is our Golden Retriever. (Remember, he was the one who often answers, "Whatever makes everyone else happy.") I (Suzette) am a strong Retriever, but also have a balanced blend of Lion, Otter, and Beaver. I tend to be the peacemaker for our family zoo.

B is for Beaver

Unlike the let's-have-a-good-time Otter, Beavers work slowly and methodically, with great attention to detail. "Quality is job one" to the industrious Beaver.

Their beds have hospital corners, their closets are arranged in alphabetical order (blouses to vests), and if they're old enough to write, there is sure to be a "to do" list prominently displayed. They are highly analytical, which can be both a strength and a weakness, depending on the situation.

Beavers have something in common with Lions. Both types can be the most insensitive of the parenting animals when pushed to an extreme. A Beaver parent can be too demanding and harsh, literally destroying the self-esteem of his or her offspring. A Beaver's children may attempt to escape the overly rigid atmosphere with drugs, alcohol, or compulsive behavior such as anorexia or bulimia. Similarly, Lion parents, if untempered, can blast their children's self-concept to smithereens.

BIBLE "ANIMALS"

We're sometimes asked after a presentation of these four personality types, "What personality type was Jesus?" The answer is simple: "All of the above." He had the most amazing personality ever.

For instance, we see the Lion side of Christ when He roared into the temple and sent the moneychangers scurrying out of His Father's house (Matthew 21:12-16). He obviously was an Otter who was invited to parties (John 2:2-11) and told entertaining yet convicting parables (Matthew 13:1-52). His Retriever side is seen in His compassion for the crowds and His tears at the tomb of His friend Lazarus (John 11:1-44). Finally, His Beaver side is showcased in His careful organization at the feeding of the five thousand: He divided the crowd into groups for distribution and even organized an efficient cleanup committee (Matthew 14:13-21).

His disciples, on the other hand, were just human beings as we are. Each of them had his own unique mix of personality traits, but it's not hard to see individual tendencies toward one "animal" type. For example, the apostle Paul had a strong Lion tendency. Even in prison Paul took charge. When the guard came to release him, Paul demanded that the guard tell the officers to come and personally escort him and Silas through the prison doors.

The apostle Peter was probably an Otter. He was outspoken and opinionated: "Hey, even if everybody else denies You, I won't!" Certainly whacking off the ear of the high priest's servant—while surrounded by temple troops—was just a bit impulsive. And walking on water was something an Otter would have tried—if only once.

Gentle John had a lot of Golden Retriever in him. We see him leaning against Jesus' chest at the Last Supper. We read it in the loving, relationship-centered book of 1 John. The intimacy John feels as he refers to "my dear children" (1 John 2:1) endears him to others.

Luke appears to have had a lot of Beaver in him. "Many have undertaken to draw up an account of the things that have been fulfilled among us, just as they were handed down to us by those who from the first were eyewitnesses and servants of the word. Therefore, since I myself have carefully investigated everything from the beginning, it seemed good also to me to write an orderly account for you" (Luke 1:1-3).

Phrases like "draw up an account," "eyewitnesses," "carefully investigated everything," and "orderly account" are all Beaverish terms.

BALANCING THE SPECIES

The purpose of examining the four personality types is not so that we can justify our immature behavior. "Hey, I'm a Lion; I can't help it if I prowl around growling and snarling at people!" Rather, we want to discover our areas of weakness so that we can conform closer to Christ's image.

I've noticed that as people allow trials to work for good in their lives, they begin to become more balanced—closer to the ideal balanced pattern that He would desire. The book of 2 Peter reminds us of God's desire for us to be balanced. Try to pick out the family animal types in this section of Scripture.

> His divine power has given us everything we need for life and godliness through our knowledge of him who called us by his own glory and goodness. Through these he has given us his very great and precious promises, so that through them you may participate in the divine nature and escape the corruption in the world caused by evil desires.
>
> For this very reason, make every effort to add to your faith, goodness; and to goodness, knowledge; and to knowledge, self-control; and to self-control, perseverance; and to perseverance, godliness; and to godliness, brotherly kindness; and to brotherly kind-ness, love. For if you possess these qualities in increas-ing measure, they will keep you from being ineffective and unproductive. (2 Peter 1:3-8)

Did you recognize some of our animals in those verses? Lions excel in perseverance. Golden Retrievers pulsate with brotherly kindness and love. Beavers are unsurpassed when it comes to self-control.

But we certainly can't allow ourselves to rationalize, "I'm an Otter, so I shouldn't be expected to show self-control." God's plan is that we develop in all areas through our interaction with Him and His children.

For instance, when Jim took a personality test ten years ago, he scored as a very high Otter and a very low Lion. He thought, *Lord, help! I am going to be a principal and school administrator, and I'm not much of a Lion. I'm in trouble!* So Jim has worked on that area. Through various life experiences and specific practice in this area, he has upped his Lion scale so he can hold his ground when the situation demands it.

So don't think that your current score will be your profile forever; remember that personality tests are simply a freeze frame or snapshot of one's behavior pattern at that particular point in time. We need to continue growing and changing to be more balanced. Character is established through the choices we make throughout our lives. While our personality is largely formed at birth, our character is shaped in the crucible of life's trials. When the combination of personality and character is molded by a commitment to Christ, we gain the godly character traits listed in 2 Peter. Such character development is a lifelong process.

EMBRACING THE WHOLE ZOO

Jesus was able to respond appropriately to each type of audience and situation. Just as He was fully God and fully Man, He was the perfect blend of positive Lion, Otter, Retriever, and Beaver qualities. The authors of the book *Perfect Love* say, Jesus had the only perfect personality! And that is why all of us are needed to accurately reflect the body of Jesus. The strengths of my temperament will offset your weaknesses. Where I am weak, others are strong.[3]

Because Jesus has the perfect blend of temperaments, He can relate to each of us right where we are in our process. With the Otterish, impulsive Peter, Christ was direct and to the point (showing His Lion trait) when He upbraided him over a suggestion that wouldn't fit with God's plan: "Get behind Me, Satan! You are a stumbling block to Me; for you are not setting your mind on God's interests, but man's" (Matthew 16:23, NASB). How's that for blunt?

When the Beaver-like Pharisees wanted the woman caught in adultery stoned ("In the Law Moses commanded us to stone such women"), Jesus bared His Lion teeth and calmly said, "If any one of you is without sin, let him be the first to throw a stone at her" (John 8:3-11). Martha, Beaverishly preoccupied with too many details, was gently reprimanded by Jesus. He commended her sister, Mary, who simply sat at His feet and listened (Luke 10:40-41).

Jesus showed His Otter side when He went fishing with His disciples and when He attended a wedding at Cana in Galilee (John 2:1). Jesus knew how to have fun with His friends! He also expressed His gentleness to John the Retriever by putting His arm around the beloved disciple at the Last Supper (John 13:23-25). And with the organizational skills of the Beaver, Jesus took twelve men and discipled them for three years. This still impacts us over two thousand years later.

Jesus adapted His interactions with others according to the needs of each individual situation. In the same way, we parents need to respond to our children in an appropriate way based on their individual temperaments. Like the modern zoo, we must not cage them with our expectations but give them freedom to become the unique individuals God created them to be.

Now that we've had a brief orientation to the four-animal system of personality typing and you've had a chance to see where you and your kids score on the various scales, let's get right into it. As you read more about the Lion trait in the next chapter, give some thought as to who around you is strongly endowed with this attribute. You'll gain new insight into the behavior of your spouse, kids, parents, coworkers, and a host of other people in your life—not the least of which is you!

THINKING IT OVER

1. What personality traits, whether obvious or subtle, become evident when you are on a family outing? Try to name at least one trait for each member of the family.
2. How does each person in your family respond when under pressure?
3. What was the root cause of the last parent/child conflict you experienced? Can you think of a way it could be handled better next time, especially in light of the personality types?
4. On a scale of one to ten (where one represents no conflict and ten represents constant conflict), how is your relationship with each of your children? With your spouse?

Notes
1. This test and the four-animal concept in general are adapted from Gary Smalley and John Trent, *The Two Sides of Love* (Pomona, Calif.: Focus on the Family, 1990), p. 35.
2. Another view of the Performax system (especially the biblical aspect) is found in (both book and workbook) *Understanding How Others Misunderstand You* (Chicago: Moody, 1990), by Ken Voges and Ron Braund.
3. Jimmy Johnson and James Watkins, *Perfect Love* (Indianapolis: Wesley, 1987), p. 52.

PART TWO

UNDERSTANDING YOUR ANIMALS

CHAPTER THREE
Taming Your Lion

A HOSPITAL CALL BUTTON IS A DANGEROUS WEAPON IN THE hands of a Lion. When Travis was in the hospital—with double pneumonia—he had the nurses constantly on the run.

"More 7-Up®!"

"I need my pillow fluffed."

"When do I get to go home?" (I'm sure the entire staff prayed it would be soon.)

Lions are not patient patients. They want to be in charge of everything—including pneumonia! They say to themselves, *I'm gonna get over this, get out of this bed, and walk out of here.*

And it didn't get any better when Travis came home from the hospital.

"Daaaaaad! Travis is just sittin' up there tellin' people what to do," my Retriever son Jason complained. "He doesn't say please or thank you or anything. He just says, 'Get it for me!'"

I tried to help Jason understand that for his Lion brother, being cooped up and not in control of his life and health was almost like torture.

BORN FREE

During the sixties a movie featuring lions in the wild made the rounds of the nation's theaters. Its theme song, "Born Free," was perfectly suited for the king of the beasts (and Lion children); they freely roam wherever they please, enjoying their kingship to the fullest.

49

As we've pointed out, there are no good or bad personality types; some are just more challenging to parents. Such
are the Lions. This inbred love of freedom is not a sign of
rebellion but a result of genetic and environmental back-
ground.

Travis's growling and snarling in the hospital was the
result of the Lion in him being caged by the illness that put
him there. But it is not just confining physical situations that
make Lions pace. Rules, curfews, restrictions—even parents
themselves—can give the Lion a case of claustrophobia. Lion
kids can be a handful for parents. The key is to recognize
when to assert your parental authority. Confrontation is more
frequently necessary with Lion kids than with other personality types. The key is to understand the Lion cub and then
direct the prowling and growling in the right direction. We'll
talk about just how to accomplish that a bit later. For now
let's continue exploring Lion characteristics.

KING OF THE JUNGLE

Lions not only need freedom, they also crave authority like
fresh-killed meat. That's why the Travises of the family zoos
are always "just sittin' up there tellin' people what to do."

John Trent told me about a friend's daughter's first day at
kindergarten. She came home from school, slammed the door
shut, threw her lunch box on the floor, and glared at her
father.

Her father, astonished, asked her what the problem was.

"I'm never going back to that school again!" she
exclaimed.

"Why not?" inquired her dad.

"Because that teacher didn't do one thing I told her to
do!" spit out the five-year-old Lioness. Strong personality
traits like this one usually show up early in life!

A Lion's penchant for claiming authority can get out of hand, but it's a good character quality when tempered correctly. Travis's soccer coach capitalized on that natural leadership quality and made Travis center midfielder. In that position, Travis functioned as a field coach. The role allowed Travis's Lion characteristics to be channeled in a positive direction. Lion-hearted people make great business executives, coaches, and political leaders. Of course, a Lion is also the most likely to become a drill sergeant or a dictator.

LIONS EAT PROBLEMS FOR BREAKFAST

Another Lion characteristic is their need for a variety of difficult challenges. For instance, one day several years ago Travis, Jason, and their friend Jared were playing with their GI-Joe® figures in the hot tub. GI-Joe was battling evil forces in the churning water, when suddenly America's hero was blown out of the water and fell unconscious behind—gasp!—the Jacuzzi. The battle ceased as the three boys stared down the narrow crack between the hot tub and the wall.

"He's gone! GI-Joe is a goner!" Jared wailed.

"Hey, have no fear! I can rescue him," Travis announced with all the authority of a five-star general.

"I don't think you can," Jason responded. "There's not even room to get a broom handle or anything in there."

"Come on, Travis, you can do it," Jared pleaded. "You've gotta save GI-Joe."

Travis climbed out of the hot tub, went into his room, and came back with a flashlight and fishing pole. Within thirty seconds, Travis had made the daring rescue and saved GI-Joe from death among the dustballs.

While challenges may frustrate—or even immobilize—

other personality types, Lions eat problems for breakfast. They love to rise to the occasion and come through with flying colors.

But it is also this love of challenges that can make Lion kids occasionally bellow out, "I'm bored!" When Travis was fourteen, he had participated in summer camp, fall football, and winter and spring basketball. The very day after basketball was over, he had been home from school only one hour when he stated emphatically, "I'm bored!"

"Can't you just relax, Travis?" his dad asked, actually as a rhetorical question. (Lions usually can't.) Fortunately, the soccer coach called the next day.

"All right, Dad! Now I can play soccer!" Travis yelled. Lion blood was once again throbbing through his teenage veins. Lions love—and indeed need—an almost constant source of challenge.

CHARGE!

Finally, Lions are hungry for advancement. Because they are the take-charge type, they love achieving goals and overcoming obstacles. But unlike the Beaver, they aren't as interested in perfection as they are in performance.

When our kids were growing up, Travis had little patience with his Retriever brother Jason and his Otter sister Jill—especially at family meetings. We tried to set goals as a family (which is a very Lionish thing to do), but Travis growled and snarled when our family meetings wandered toward silliness. "Come on, let's get on with it," he'd bellow. "Let's either do something or call this meeting adjourned!"

Patience is a skill we must help our Lion kids to learn (and sometimes we Lion parents need to learn it, too).

LION CUB MEETS THE QUEEN
OF THE JUNGLE

One of the hardest lessons for Lion children to learn is that there is a higher authority than themselves. According to them, "the buck never stops here." They don't want anyone or anything to obstruct their plans, so conflict usually arises when a line is drawn and they are told not to step over it.

When Travis was in fifth grade he met a teacher who drew not just one such line, but several. You can ask Travis today which of his teachers made an impact on his life, and Mrs. Doris Hagar is right at the top of his list. The kids nicknamed her "Hagar the Horrible" because she didn't condone any type of insubordination—subtle or overt. Imagine that! She wouldn't put up with rudeness or unkindness. She expected the best of every one of her students. She commanded, not demanded, respect.

Travis started the school year thinking he had the world on a string. His interrupting and silliness kept him in trouble the entire fall. About Christmas time he finally figured the system out: you misbehave, you suffer the consequences. After missing several recesses and writing hundreds of "I will not . . ." sentences, he realized that Mrs. Hagar meant business. She told me (Suzette) in a parent-teacher conference at midterm that she had a running sentence list for Travis in her file drawer. She had him so well grounded by the second semester that she would simply reach for the file drawer of "I will nots" and he would immediately straighten up. Travis had learned a hard lesson: He was not the one in charge.

Mrs. Hagar did something that many Lion-tempered adults fail to do when interacting with children: She let her students know by her actions and her words that she cared deeply for each one of them. She would tell Travis that she knew he would grow up to be a fine young man some day.

She told him about his good qualities, but that he would have to learn to obey the rules. We still have the letter she wrote to him the summer after his fifth grade year. She told him she saw a bright and rewarding future for him and encouraged him always to do his best. Doris Hagar died of cancer a few years later. Although she never got to see the impact she had on Travis, surely she is in heaven smiling. We will always be indebted to her for hanging in there and teaching our Lion cub what every person needs to learn: Like it or not, we are always under some authority. We may not agree with the rules, but harmony is impossible unless we abide by them.

THE COWARDLY LION

Lions may appear to be the picture of confidence, but like the famous lion from *The Wizard of Oz*, most kings of the jungle also are plagued with fear. Watch children playing table games or sports. Which are the most competitive? Hate coming in second? Right—Lions!

Lions' greatest fear is to be outperformed. That's why they're so incredibly competitive and have a tendency toward insensitivity. They have an innate need to be the captain, the first in line, the valedictorian, the CEO, the chairman of the church board, and so on. Lee Iacocca and Saddam Hussein are typical of this personality type—for good and bad.

I tried to explain this to Jason, our Retriever-hearted son, as it pertained to his brother's post-hospital behavior.

"Travis doesn't realize he's being insensitive, Jason. We have to help him see that."

Whereas Lions may see themselves as decisive and independent, others may see them as harsh and pushy. They may view themselves as determined and efficient, but everyone else may judge them as tough and domineering.

Usually it takes trials and suffering to temper a Lion's tendency toward insensitivity. And Travis has definitely had his share. We're amazed when we look back on all the accidents and illnesses he had during his growing-up years. Besides the double pneumonia, he had stitches four times, dry sockets as a result of surgery to remove his wisdom teeth, surgery on his ankle that caused him to miss basketball season his senior year of high school, a broken nose (three times!), and a ruptured appendix during his freshman year of college.

This is not to say that all Lions have these kinds of things happen to them for the purpose of character development, but everyone who has trials either develops more balance or sinks deeper into the extremes of his or her given personality type. In other words, we become bitter or better.

Through Travis's trials and testing he has become a sensitive young man. He is majoring in biology and has plans for medical school. His goal in life is to help others. He will probably be a compassionate doctor because of the physical ailments he has endured.

MOTIVATING YOUR LION

Unlike the loyal Golden Retriever, Lions don't need a lot of "warm fuzzies" and small talk to motivate them. Remember, the king of the jungle is goal oriented. He needs clear, brief instructions. "Get to the bottom line!" he often roars.

Because Lions are so achievement oriented, charts are excellent motivators for Lion kids. A check-off chart might include various tasks:

☐ Make bed each morning.
☐ Feed the cat before dark.
☐ Share your toys.

Lions at a Glance

Lions tend to like:
Freedom
Leadership roles
Competition, challenges
Goals
Reasons for doing things

Lions tend to fear:
Coming in second—in anything

Lions are motivated by:
Goals, individual achievements
Directions, not demands
Freedom to make choices
Challenges

Charts are individual records of accomplishment, which suits this personality type very well. Lions are solitary creatures who don't always participate well in team sports—unless they can be the quarterback or forward. They don't like to share the limelight—or gold stars—with others. Lions by nature also need a long leash. Because they crave freedom, they prefer choices. This is particularly challenging to parents if their first child is a Retriever or Beaver who needs and wants a very structured environment and detailed instructions.

One way to meet the Lion's need for a long leash is to give him the freedom to choose when he will do something. While a Golden Retriever wants to know the exact time to feed the cat, a Lion prefers instructions such as, "You must feed the cat anytime before bedtime—you pick the time."

Another technique is to provide a challenge with each task. (Remember, Lions love overcoming obstacles.) For instance, I (Jim) once needed to motivate Travis to rake leaves—not much of a challenge for a Lion. But our pickup truck was right where I wanted Travis to burn the leaves. What could be a better motivation for a fourteen-year-old Lion than to drive Dad's truck?

"Travis, I need you to burn the leaves after you rake them, but you'll have to move the truck first," I implored.

Travis attacked the leaves with all the enthusiasm and aggression a Lion can unleash. You would have thought I'd promised to let him drive two hundred miles to St. Louis, rather than just twenty feet. But Travis saw it as a real challenge. A young Beaver, on the other hand, would be absolutely terrified at the prospect of driving my truck. "I don't have a driver's license," a Beaver might say. "What if I can't stop it?"

Because Lions love challenges, routine tasks usually cause the Lion child to roar, "That's boring!" But Lions need to learn that some chores—no matter how boring—have to be done. They also need to learn to operate within some controls and restrictions. At the modern zoo there are still boundaries and parameters—for the safety not only of humans, but of the animals as well. Past experience has helped us discover that if the parameters are reasonable and explained to the child, he or she can still have a blast within the secure and safe environment of those boundaries.

Finally, Lions are strong-willed by nature. And when you have to stare one down, you need to have plenty of ammunition ready. Appeal to their goal orientation and show the positive or negative results if something is done or not done. Instead of just ordering them to "cease and desist" on the basis of your parental authority (which would almost surely provoke a struggle, since Lions tend to fear no one), try saying, "Travis, I can't let you do that. It's dangerous and could hurt others." That usually works out better than simply ordering a Lion about.

Most important, attack the problem not the person. Lions are hardest on themselves. They rarely need to be told when they've blown it, but parents do need to help their cub see each situation as a learning or disciplining tool for the next challenge. Though Lions are the quickest of the four animals to bounce back, sometimes it takes a little coaxing to bring them out of a funk after a real or perceived failure. Be aware of what can happen when you overreact with Lion children. Though Lion kids are tough, their spirits can be broken just as a Golden Retriever's can. After all, they're just kids, not soldiers.

Our friend Norma Smalley tries to find the good in the worst situations; she calls this "treasure hunting." In the face of a personal failure or discouragement, you can help your child find a lesson to be learned or a good thing to gain from the bad situation. Help him look for that silver lining in each dark cloud.

⊚

Next we look at the fun-loving Otter. For those of you who have either a mate or child with this predominant characteristic, you'll gain new understanding for why they act the way they do. We'll look at how they view life, why they have trouble being serious, why they are constantly distracted, and why Otter kids (not to mention Otter parents) hate to do chores. Their usually delightful personality traits can sometimes get out of hand, so we'll discuss how you can effectively parent kids blessed with this orientation.

THINKING IT OVER

1. Do you have a child who possesses the characteristics of a Lion? If not, do you know a child who does? What are his or her most obvious traits?
2. What are some challenging activities that appeal to the Lion child in your family? (If you have problems coming up with ideas, ask him or her for some.)
3. What trials has your Lion child experienced lately that caused personal pain or conflict with others? Discuss the trials with your child and how he or she can avoid this pain or conflict in the future.
4. Since these children are so goal oriented, what are some goals you can help your cub make to further his or her communication and interpersonal skills?
5. What are some key areas you can praise your Lion child for? Try to encourage your cub about at least one thing each day.
6. Now that you know more about the strengths and weaknesses of the Lion trait, think about your family members. Is there someone in your family who needs to either strengthen or tone down his Lion tendency? Do *you* need to do either?

CHAPTER FOUR
Calming Your Otter

THE RAIN BEGAN TO LET UP AS I (JIM) WAS HEADED TOWARD TOWN with Jill following me in her car. We were on our "date" night—an evening we've set aside each week for years. At seventeen Jill still looks forward to this time we spend together. As we drove west the clouds began to break and a beautiful sunset was in the making. Being a former science teacher, I realized there would be a brilliant rainbow if I just looked to the east. And there it was! Not one, but two full rainbows on the horizon. In my excitement I rolled down my window and pointed toward them so Jill would see. I pulled over and she followed. We wouldn't have missed savoring the moment before scurrying off to Jill's restaurant of choice and enjoying an evening full of conversation and renewal.

The spontaneity of that moment reflects our personal bond. Jill and I have been adventurous rainbow-chasers all our lives. We dream out loud to those around us. We take risks. We often fail to think through the consequences of our actions. But boy, do we have fun!

If you've seen otters in a zoo, then you know that these fun-loving creatures personify perpetual motion. Into the water. Out of the water. Back into the water. Swimming in dizzying circles. Eating while floating on their backs and balancing their food on their stomachs. (Does that sound like one of your children? Your spouse? You?)

A popular television commercial features the Energizer® Bunny—a battery-powered rabbit who bursts into other commercials with its drum-pounding performance. That bunny is a lot like our daughter. She's a nuclear-powered bundle of optimism and emotional energy—she "just keeps going, and going, and going. . . ."

Otters don't need to be reminded that their ideas won't always work or that something is too risky. Either consequences or the reality of the situation is usually obvious and brings them back down to earth. Sometimes with a thud.

ALL THEY WANNA DO IS HAVE SOME FUN

Several years ago we went skiing in Colorado. Jill took to snow like an otter to water. She could out-ski Suzette and me—even without poles. Jill skied a bit with us, then got bored and darted down the slope by herself.

"Jill, don't get that far ahead of . . ." Suzette started to say, but by then Jill had disappeared into the blowing snow.

"Jim," Suzette panted, "I can't see her." By then the wind had turned the slope and sky into a white swirl. We felt our way along the trail—until it forked in two different directions.

"Which way did she go?" I asked, not expecting an answer. Both trails were blown over, covering any evidence of recent tracks.

"Jim, it's getting dark. What are we going to do?"

"Okay, which trail would an Otter take?" I asked out loud.

"The most dangerous one," Suzette snapped, obviously losing patience with her two Otters.

"This one looks the most interesting, Suzette. It sort of weaves in and out of the woods. I'll take it, and you take the other one." I started to thread my way through the trees as darkness began to overtake the mountain.

"Jill! Jill!" I hollered. There in the blue glow of snowy twilight was Jill—straddling a tree off to the side of the trail.

"Hey, look what I did, Dad!" She laughed. I heaved a sigh of relief.

For Jill, life is a continual sitcom. She really began to laugh when I took off my skis to try to untangle her skis from the trees. As I stepped off the trail, my two-hundred-pound, six-foot body sank chest deep into the powdery snow. I managed to free her, only to watch her disappear down the trail and leave me struggling in six feet of snow. I can tell you, that wasn't fun at all.

Jill didn't realize the danger she could have been in if she'd been lost for hours, or that I could have died from frostbite if left out overnight in a snowdrift. One of the challenges, then, of raising Otters is to instill in them healthy boundaries. "Boundary" is a dirty word to Otters, but it's something they have to learn.

"I want you to know one thing, Jill," I said after finally managing to crawl on my stomach over the soft snow to the trail, get my skis back on, and grope my way back to the lodge. "This is where your adventurous spirit got you into trouble. Big trouble. From now on, you never go down a trail without someone else!"

Even in her Otterish exuberance, Jill nodded solemnly in agreement. She had seen a glimpse of the potentially tragic consequences of unrestricted Otterish behavior.

DOING WHAT YOU OTTER

It's probably a dangerous thing to have an Otter as a camp director. But I (Jim) have learned—along with Jill—that sometimes it's best to stifle your Otter and do what you ought to. Doing the right thing is tough medicine for Otters, but they eventually learn it's good for them. I've learned to temper my Otterish urges, especially when it comes to the safety of others.

One incident about fifteen years ago illustrates this lesson. To me it seemed like a great idea. Sure, it had rained all night, but that shouldn't put a damper on taking fifteen college-age camp counselors canoeing and kayaking, should it? Okay, the water was running about a foot above the bridges along the river, but that would just make it more fun. I put these eager counselors, who had come to camp early for work week, in Swan Creek at 9:00 A.M. and then drove down to the midway point to take pictures of the colorful scene. Or so I thought.

Thirteen inches of rain that month had turned this normally peaceful stretch of water into a raging, storm-swollen Amazon. Treetops were sticking up from the surface of the water, and the bridges were creating dangerous undercurrents. As I arrived at the viewing point, I saw ten of the thirteen craft floating along—empty! They had capsized in the rough water. I saw several terrified counselors clinging to tree branches.

After realizing the danger these kids were in due to my miscalculation and impulsiveness, I kept saying to myself, *Brawner, this is crazy! You get excited about something, and then you don't weigh the consequences or really look at the details.* What had started out as a three-hour adventure ended up an eleven-hour nightmare. Thankfully we were able recover all the counselors and canoes and kayaks. Through this experience and others I've learned my lesson regarding letting my Otter side run wild.

Sometimes we forget that in reality all of us have all four traits within our personality to draw from. This became clear to me one day while I was in Colorado working at one of our *Love Is a Decision* seminars.

Gary Smalley, who is an incurable Otter, woke up one morning and enthusiastically suggested we jog to the top of one of the nearby mountains. (Otters are often morning people, to the dismay of others.) Now keep in mind that in the spring, the mountains are like tundra—thawed out just enough to create muddy quicksand that sucks at your shoes. So there we were: John Trent, me, and Terry Brown, huffing and puffing behind Gary in the thin Colorado air, flipping mud all over our bodies with every stride. And all the time Gary is exclaiming, "Isn't this great!" He was not receiving hearty "amens" in return, but in his enthusiasm, he didn't notice.

I was muttering under my breath, *This is really dumb. Why are we doing this, anyway? I've just ruined a brand-new pair of running shoes! My clothes are so muddy, how will I ever get them in my suitcase to take them home?*

But I found the treasure in the situation. I realized in one of those muddy moments that I was getting my blend of traits under control. I smiled to myself and thought, *Hey, I'm not a total Otter after all!*

SHINE THE SPOTLIGHT ON ME, PLEASE

Otters draw part of their energy from being in the spotlight. They're natural entertainers. We (Suzette and Jill) had an "Otter Heaven" experience one spring on prom day. Jill had an appointment to get her nails done at one beauty salon and her hair done at another. It was to be a full day of pampering and primping, and the #1 Otter could not have been more excited.

After two hours at the nail salon we headed to Gary's Coiffures, the largest and busiest salon in town. It is similar to the beauty shop in the movie *Steel Magnolias*; if it's happening in town, you can get the latest scoop there. When we came through the door I knew we would be there for several hours. At least ten other girls planning to attend the Buccaneer Ball were already being shampooed, made up, and painted. Jill's appointment took all of twenty-five minutes. She looked like a princess. However, more fun than looking like a princess was the process of visiting each beauty station to see how everyone else was having their hair fixed, learning what times their dates were picking them up and asking where they were being taken for dinner.

After I finally convinced Jill that we really needed to go, she asked if we could visit yet another shop where she knew several other girls had appointments. We spent another forty-five minutes checking out the progress of her other friends—as well as friends she had never met before. Otters love to make new friends, and Jill made several new ones that day. On the way home I was hoping that the actual prom would be as fun as the day we had spent getting ready.

Although Otters tend to have many acquaintances, they're often content to leave their relationships at a shallow level. They are frequently more interested in an audience—small or large—than in a deep friendship. If you could listen in on a conversation between Otters at a party, for example, you'd find that Otters tend to limit themselves to a social "script":

"Hi, I'm John Otter. And you are?"

"Hi, I'm Jane Otter."

"Great party, isn't it?"

"Yeah."

"What school do you go to?"

"Wetlands Junior High. I'm in seventh grade."

"Really. I go there, too. Well, great to get to know you. See ya around."

By the end of the party Otters can recognize the faces of those they've talked to but have probably forgotten names, grades, and anything else about the people they have met.

It's extremely important to encourage your Otter to develop deeper, more meaningful relationships so he or she will be able to connect more effectively with the other three personalities. This can be accomplished by appealing to your Otter's "hot button"—her sociability. The goal is to help the Otter perceive relationships in a light that is familiar to her personality and that will give her a platform to nurture new friendships.

Because social interaction is high on an Otter's list of priorities, encourage activities that will involve your Otter with the three other distinct personality types. An Otter might interact with a Beaver by playing a game of Monopoly or Scrabble. With a Lion, a more physical game like tag or red-light-green-light might be the ticket. To the Retriever, a card game or board game like Life that isn't highly competitive might be more appealing.

THE PEOPLE-LOVERS

Like her father and grandmother, Jill loves to interact with anyone and everyone. My (Jim's) mom is always so busy enjoying her family that it's practically a Thanksgiving and Christmas tradition for her to forget the rolls baking in the oven—until black smoke pours out from the oven door to remind her. She also lost a few potholders by setting them on the burner while the pilot light was on.

Otters are not as forgetful and disorganized as they are fun-oriented, so much so that details are low on their list of priorities. And it's their people-loving personality that makes an Otter such a beloved and noisy animal. People generally love to be around Otters. But that noise factor can sometimes get out of hand, especially with kids.

For instance, Jill could always hold her own to the "snap-crackle-popping" of five bowls of cereal with her constant chatter. One morning at the breakfast table Travis complained, "Jill, will you just pipe down? You're going to have all your words used up before breakfast!"

I (Jim) realized I needed to step into the fray. "Both of you need to call a truce right now and try to understand one another," I said, trying to avert another breakfast battle. "Travis, I know chitchat really rattles your cage, but just back off. I think you owe your sister an apology for your rude remark." Travis acknowledged his rudeness and solemnly asked Jill's forgiveness. Then I turned to Jill and said, "I realize you love to talk, but you have only ten more words until breakfast is over." Silence reigned for a few moments.

In the uneasy silence of the cease-fire, I tried to help both Travis and Jill understand each other.

"Jill, you see yourself as personable and outgoing, but Travis may see you as too talkative or somewhat controlling." Her brother nodded in agreement.

I continued, "You think you're enthusiastic, but your brothers might think you're obnoxious. You view yourself as dramatic, but they may see you as spacey."

Jill stared at her cereal. Otters are usually thin-skinned, so I tried to encourage our little pup. "But that's okay, Jill," I said stroking her long blonde hair. "People aren't always going to understand you—or Jason, or Travis, or even me. I love you just the way you are. In time, little by little, you'll understand how you can make the best connection with those you relate to every day."

MOTIVATING YOUR OTTER

Because Otters like to influence others, they need to feel involved with decisions. Whenever possible, get them in on the discussion and plotting stages of whatever you're planning with or for them. If they believe they have had a say in the plan, it will be easier for them to carry it out—whether it's a vacation or rules or consequences for behavior. We'll see

Otters at a Glance

Otters tend to like:
Anything fun

Opportunities to help and/or motivate others

A platform to inform or entertain others

Otters tend to fear:
Deadlines

Boring activities

Rejection

Otters are motivated by:
Recognition and approval

Fun

Challenges

how Otters can contribute to family goal setting in chapter 12. Otters are usually strong self-motivators, so one of the secrets to motivating them is simply not to *de*motivate them. If you're an all-business style parent (which Lion kids love), you'll probably turn off an Otter. Take time to relate to him and affirm him before handing him a list of chores. And try to lighten up and have some fun; you'll communicate better with your young Otter, and who knows—you might even enjoy life a little more yourself!

A friend of ours, Mike, appeals to his nine-year-old Otter daughter by planning a "date" with her. As she completes her list of chores, she gets to choose the restaurant or the evening's activity. She gets to go on a date with Dad no matter what, but if she can get most or all of the list completed, she gets to choose the activity. Otters love a wide array of choices, so Mike's approach with his daughter is highly motivating.

Keep in mind, too, that Otters' emotions tend to be extreme. When they're up, they're really up. But when they're down, they're down and out. Because of this they're easily discouraged.

For instance, when Jill was ten she was enjoying a new toy that splatters small amounts of paint on a piece of paper as it spins at a high speed. The art that results resembles multicolor suns with the rays spreading out from the center. I was busy writing when Jill brought me one of her creations, and I wasn't in the mood to do an art critique on what looked like an explosion at a paint factory. Fortunately I caught myself before I crushed her spirit and ruined her motivation by saying something like, "Later, Jill! Can't you see I'm busy?"

Instead I affirmed, "Jill, that's really neat!" And then I tried a technique called *redirecting*. "You know, what you need to do is make one of these beautiful paintings for each member of the family. How 'bout making them in everyone's favorite colors? And then sign them just like expensive art."

"That's a great idea, Dad," Jill responded and then eagerly went back to her room. I was back to work in less than thirty seconds, and Jill was kept busy—and motivated—for another thirty minutes.

We've also tried to appeal to the Otter side of our children by making chores into a game. For instance, chopping wood is not exactly in the same league of entertainment as Nintendo®. But I (Jim) tried to make the chore as exciting as a television game show. I would announce to our teenage boys, "I can split that piece in two swings." Then the kids would start calling their shots, the winner being the one who called the number of swings correctly. There were no cash prizes or trips to Hawaii, but a trip to the frozen yogurt store was a great motivation. Travis and Jason ended up loving to chop wood.

With a little bit of creativity, you can make most any task fun. For instance, while director of overnight trips at Kanakuk Kamp, I always dreaded blowing up my air mattress. One day as I was feeling light-headed huffing and puffing into the mattress, it dawned on me: *Why should I blow this thing up?* With enthusiasm in my voice I asked the group of eight-, nine-, and ten-year-olds, "Kids, who wants to blow up my air mattress?" Before I knew it there were six in line waiting to huff and puff on my behalf.

At home, we even made washing dishes more exciting. Jill created suds creatures in the soap froth floating on the water. Now, you have to be careful with Otters because they can make a mess of things. But if you can make a chore fun, a challenge, or something the child can take pride in, then you've successfully motivated him or her.

Even discipline can be turned into something fun. On one spring break, we decided to take the family on a vacation to the Canadian Rockies. We had flown into Seattle and were going to rent a minivan for the trip into the mountains. After a long flight, the Brawner zoo was starting to erupt in grumblings akin to feeding time at the Lion exhibit. I left Suzette with the kids and went to the rental counter for our van. However, because the NCAA basketball play-offs were in town, all the vans were taken. When I arrived outside baggage claim in an intermediate-sized car, the growling and snarling erupted into animal Armageddon.

"That's it! I've had enough," I said. "Travis and Jill, you are going to hug each other until your mom and I get all this luggage stuffed into this car." Two pairs of eyes stared in disbelief—along with several strangers waiting at the curb.

"Hug!" I bellowed. "And don't let go till I say so!"

Travis and Jill slowly obeyed. Other passengers set their suitcases down to watch this family drama. After several minutes our Siamese twins began to shake and weave with laughter, and soon harmony was restored. We still talk and laugh about that scene.

Because they are so social, Otters hate to feel left out. When they are misbehaving in a group, a time-out away from the action is a strong incentive not to repeat their wrong.

Fun rewards are also strong motivators: "If you'll help with such-and-such, then we'll be able to go to such-and-such an event." Just remember that if you attach rewards to performance, you need to follow through. I realize that for Beaver- or Lion-oriented parents, this may sound like too much fun. But it's important to respect our child's personality and work with it as a given, not as something that can or should be dramatically changed.

@

Otter children can be a challenge—and a delight—for parents. Golden Retrievers present a different set of issues to understand and deal with. "Man's best friend" can bring a glowing warmth to your home. He or she can also be overly sensitive and easily hurt. In either case, the next chapter will teach you how better to communicate with and love the Golden Retriever in your family circle.

THINKING IT OVER

1. Can you identify anyone in your family who seems to be an Otter? Does he or she enjoy having fun and taking risks? Does this person have a problem keeping his room clean? Do you constantly have to remind her not to forget this or that? How do you react to him? Do you find yourself disliking her behavior (even if only slightly)? Has this chapter helped you to see his orientation in a more favorable (or at least more neutral) light?
2. What are some games your Otter child likes to play? Can you think of any games you could create that would help him or her accomplish chores or duties? What rewards or deterrents would motivate him or her to act responsibly? What are some creative reminders that would help your Otter remember tasks such as finishing homework, picking up clothes, and finding hats or glasses?
3. When an Otter child is excited and out of control, it's important for you to remain calm. In such a situation, what could you do to bring things back under control?
4. Because of their nature, Otter's need at least one good affirming comment from their parents each day. What have you praised your Otter for today?
5. Now that you see the strengths and weaknesses of the Otter, think about your family members. Who in your family needs either to strengthen or tone down his Otter tendency? Do *you* need to do either?

CHAPTER FIVE

Reassuring Your Golden Retriever

As we write this, our son Jason is a grown man and towers over me (Suzette) at six feet, four inches tall. But not so long ago (as we parents so often muse) he was only five. Jason was playing in his room (I thought) when I suddenly became aware that the house was awfully quiet. (Know the feeling? The peace feels good at first, but then panic threatens as you begin to imagine where your kids could be or what mischief they have gotten into.) I realized I hadn't seen Jason in about half an hour, and I searched frantically through the house to no avail. He was gone.

I dashed to the window and scanned the backyard, then to the front of the house, where I glimpsed him near the street, sitting down on the curb. Praying desperately that he wouldn't go into the street before I could reach him, I ran out front. When I got close enough to assess the situation, I slowed down as I overheard my little boy.

Jason was holding a carrot (which he had evidently pilfered from the refrigerator) and talking to a dead squirrel. The poor creature had been squashed by a car, and Jason was trying to revive it

"Here ya go, little feller—here's some food so you can feel better," intoned my son. "Eat the carrot, 'cuz Mommy says vegt'bls is good for you."

My quiet chuckling soon turned to welled-up tears of love for God's gracious gift to our family: sensitive and compassionate Jason, our Golden Retriever.

If you or one of your children has Retriever qualities, you know it. Retrievers are easy to spot because they're more interested in relationships than goals (Lions), a good time (Otters), or tasks (Beavers). Golden Retrievers thrive on interacting with other people.

At first glance, Retrievers may not appear to be "people people." At the same party where an Otter is scurrying around meeting everyone, a Retriever is usually off in the corner spending time with just one or two people. By the end of the evening, the Retriever can tell you all the "vital statistics" about those one or two people, as well as their favorite subject and teacher, whether their mom and dad are getting along, who they have a crush on, their favorite music group, and many more details. While Otters tend to have many surface friendships, Retrievers usually have only a few deep relationships. Golden Retrievers make terrific friends and spouses—you can count on them to be there for you when you need them.

A HEART WITH LEGS

Self-sacrifice is a Retriever's middle name. And our oldest child is the epitome of the Retriever personality. At twenty-three, Jason is a graphic artist and designer. In his spare time he's a volunteer fireman for the local county fire protection district and makes several calls each week with his unit. His wife, Alison, is a kindergarten teacher. Jason frequently assists Alison on field trips and special activities with her class. Her students treat him like a big teddy bear—towering over them, he's a "heart with legs."

Rewind the tape! As a fifth grader, Jason was one of the friendliest kids you could imagine. Even then he was a head taller than most of his classmates, but he certainly didn't fit the stereotype of "big kid equals bully." After school had begun in the fall of that year I (Suzette) noticed that Jason's wardrobe was shrinking. Since Retrievers can be forgetful and often misplace personal items, I began to question and backtrack where he'd been so I could reclaim his "lost" clothing.

By thorough investigation, I made an enlightening and heartwarming discovery through Jason's teacher. Jason had noticed a friend at school had been wearing the same clothes almost every day. He also knew that this friend's family was not doing well financially. Jason started putting a few of his clothes in a grocery sack every couple of weeks and then giving them to his teacher, who would place them in this student's locker. Jason discretely and purposefully connected in a characteristically Retriever manner. The joy he gained was seeing his friend wear new clothes as a result of a random and anonymous act of kindness. (Most Retrievers are guilty of this.)

You may have been the beneficiary of such an act. Retrievers don't want recognition for their kindness; they only want to see someone else have a little joy or success. As adults, these people keep the greeting card business prosperous and the Girl Scout cookie drive alive and thriving.

STEADY AS SHE GOES

Not only do Retrievers want deep, secure relationships, but they also hunger for daily patterns and consistent, familiar surroundings. They don't generally adjust well to change—such as a move to another town, a divorce, a new school, or even the addition of a new sibling to the family. They tend to thrive on routine and predictability; they are truly creatures of habit.

Again, that can be either positive or negative. The positive side is dependability; the negative side is resistance to change—even positive change. Retrievers often grow up to be the church board member whose favorite line is, "We've never done it that way before. Why should we change now?"

Part of the reason Retrievers dislike change is because

they are intensely loyal to people. A geographical move threatens relationships with people they have come to depend on and from whom they draw emotional energy.

For instance, when Suzette and I moved from Harrison to Little Rock, Arkansas, we went from a rural community to a fast-paced metropolitan area. Suzette took a teaching job to supplement our income. This also meant four-year-old Jason and two-year-old Travis had to attend a preschool. Travis couldn't wait to get to class for all the activities. But for Jason, every morning when he was "left" at the school was a traumatic experience. Jason felt he had been deserted by his mother and by his own brother, who was off having a ball with other kids.

The entire year created anxiety and stress for Jason, who had been ripped away from his hometown, his mother, and Travis. We knew we had to do something different to provide Jason with a more consistent and controlled environment, so Suzette started a gymnastics school. This allowed her to schedule her work hours to spend more time with the boys and give Jason the stability he needed. That was one of the best decisions we ever made. Kids desperately need consistency and security, and I believe parents should move mountains to provide all the support we can—especially during those early years—regardless of our kids' personality mix.

NO SUDDEN TURNS, PLEASE

Disrupted relationships are difficult for Golden Retrievers to handle, and unexpected change of any type is also tough. That's why it's important to preview any change well in advance and allow Retrievers to process the pertinent information. Then introduce the actual change at a later date, when appropriate.

A few years ago, I (Jim) was being interviewed by a company in another state. Since this would have meant relocation for our family, Suzette and I kept the details to ourselves, not wanting to upset our children unduly (especially if I ended up not taking the position). This was especially true for Jason, who was thirteen at the time.

During the latter stages of our consideration process, I began to prepare Jason for the actual family discussion of this critical decision by asking leading questions: "Do you think my talents are being used to their fullest?" and "Are you able to visualize me ever doing any other work?" Then when we actually shared the opportunity at a family meeting, we asked questions such as, "How do you think this decision would affect you?" and "What opportunities do you see in this new situation?" and "What are the pros and cons of this decision from your point of view?"

Having prepped Jason for this discussion with both advance warning (Retrievers like to mull things over) and probing questions undoubtedly helped him process the information involved in the decision. As it turned out, I ended up not accepting the offer, but Suzette and I learned the value of preparing our kids and allowing them to have a part in the decision-making process.

DON'T RUSH ME

Because of their need for familiar patterns, Retrievers don't make quick decisions—or, for that matter, do anything quickly. For instance, Jason always punched the snooze button on his alarm clock two or three times before getting up. Travis, on the other hand, was out of the bed, had it made, and was in the shower before the alarm's sound waves had reached his brother. That's why we had different wake-up times for each of our children. We gave Jason lots of time because the more you pressure a Retriever to hurry, the slower he becomes. Our goal was to get everyone ready at the same time, even though they didn't start at the same time. Allowing for our kids' individual differences saved much frustration.

MOTIVATING YOUR GOLDEN RETRIEVER

Because Golden Retrievers tend to be peacemakers and followers, they can be easily intimidated by Lions, especially if the Lion is their parent. For example, one woman we know has a strong Retriever daughter, Valerie, who hardly ever gets out of hand. In contrast, her younger brother is a bundle of energy and a mischievous child who often needs correction. The mother is amazed that when she verbally corrects Valerie's little brother in front of her, Valerie straightens up her act, too. The little Retriever is so eager to please that even though it's clear the reproof is not directed at her, she tries even harder to obey. And if her little brother is disciplined, Valerie is often moved to tears. Why? Strong feelings of empathy. This behavior is typical of Golden Retrievers. They often side with the underdog.

Such extreme sensitivity can either be a blessing or a curse, depending on its level and the mix with other personality traits. Regardless of the mix, as parents we need to remember that nurturing our children is "job one."

Golden Retrievers tend to be good listeners, but often parents have to draw them out by asking them questions and soliciting their opinions. Then we can hear and see what they're really feeling, rather than carrying on a conversation with ourselves because they're such good listeners. And we need to learn to hear between the lines. Suzette, having a strong get-to-the-point Lion tendency, had to learn to be sensitive to Jason's pace and way of processing information.

Golden Retrievers at a Glance

Golden Retrievers tend to like:
A few deep friendships
Regular, predictable patterns in
daily life
Clearly defined rules and goals

Golden Retrievers tend to fear:
Unplanned changes
The unknown
Loss of stability

Golden Retrievers are motivated by:
Loyalty to people and programs
Acceptance by others

Instead of pelting him with a quick "How was your day?" she spent time sitting beside his bed before lights-out. When he was younger, she would lie down beside him and give him the time he needed.

She was also careful not to close Jason off by expressing anger or shock at something he said. She allowed herself to feel those emotions when appropriate, but she tried not to express them around tenderhearted Jason. The best strategy is to hold those feelings inside until you get to your room where you can scream into your pillow. After you've calmed down a bit, you can bring up the subject again and talk calmly about it with your Retriever pup.

⊚

Now let's turn from the gentle and cooperative Golden Retriever to the somewhat more demanding Beaver. Beavers have high standards—for themselves and others. If you have a child (or a mate) who's hard on herself or who tends toward perfectionism, you'll be especially interested in the next chapter.

THINKING IT OVER

1. Do you have a Retriever child (or know of one) who bonds tightly to one friend—sometimes even to the exclusion of others? What is it about his personality that makes him or her so loyal? Do you view this as an asset or a liability? Why?

2. Why do you think a Golden Retriever usually has problems starting and completing tasks? Can you think of some relational methods that would motivate him or her in this area?

3. When reproving or disciplining a Retriever, have you ever noticed his nonverbal communication (for example,

body language and facial expression)? What do you think his or her personality orientation has to do with such signals?

4. Have you experienced the crushing of a Retriever's spirit under harsh discipline? Can you think of softer, more effective ways you could motivate him or her to change undesirable behavior?

5. In this chapter were you able to see the strengths and weaknesses of the Golden Retriever personality? Who in your family needs to either strengthen or tone down his or her Golden Retriever tendency? Do *you* need to do either?

CHAPTER SIX

Loving Your Beaver

THE KICKING COACH WALKED UP TO OUR MIDDLE CHILD AFTER HIS second game of the season. Travis handles all the kicking for his college football team at Southwest Missouri State University. A bit distraught over missing a field goal in the last game, Travis was mulling over how he could change his kicking style to avoid that same mistake in the future. His analytical nature had the best of him.

Travis inquired of his coach, "What do you think I'm doing that needs to be corrected? Is it my approach? The angle of the placement? Or just plain—"

Coach interrupted Travis in mid-sentence. "Travis, how are you on extra points?"

"Six out of six," he replied.

"How about field goals?" Coach continued.

"Three out of four."

"If my math holds true, that would be nine out of a possible ten. Travis, I wouldn't change a thing!"

Yet after a recent game in which he made two of three attempts on field goals, Travis was quoted in the newspaper as saying, "Anything less than perfect is unacceptable."

PERFECTION: EVERY BEAVER'S GOAL

Our Lion has plenty of Beaver in him. Beavers have high expectations of themselves and others. They have a built-in need to "get it right." Beavers will recopy an entire writing assignment if they smudge one word. They'll white out mistakes in their private journals—documents that no one else will ever see. "It matters to me," they say. And multiple-choice tests are especially difficult because they want to be sure they've picked the *best* answer.

Their need for perfection usually causes them to take much more time to accomplish a task than other personality types. Therefore, they can sometimes be oblivious to time. They also lose a lot of sleep, since getting an assignment right is more important than getting enough rest. My guess is that Beavers also take much longer to date and get married than other personality types. I don't have scientific proof for this one, but there is a lot of anecdotal evidence that even in personal relationships Beavers like to take their time and do it right.

Because of their perfectionist tendencies, Beavers may be the hardest of the personality types to relate to. Whereas they perceive themselves as thorough and industrious, others may see them as critical and picky. Whereas they think of themselves as serious, others may see them as uptight and even moralistic. Other personality types—particularly Otters—see the Beaver's need for orderliness as compulsive and obsessive. Otters can see almost no reason at all to be as careful, thorough, and precise as Beavers usually are—but that's as much a statement on Otters as on Beavers.

If Beavers let their perfectionism run wild in their view of and approach to life, they can create an endless treadmill of misery for themselves. Why? Well, depending on your personality mix, you may or may not understand this point. The other three personality types have never adopted perfection as a realistic and achievable goal in life, but strong Beavers actually believe that they *can* attain perfection in practically all they do, and they endlessly chase that carrot on a stick. But life is not really like that, so we need to help Beavers become more realistic and accepting of their human limitations. High standards are great, but perfection is impossible.

CAUTION: THE BEAVER'S BYWORD:

Beaver children can drive parents bananas with their extreme caution. For example, the child may get a new bike for Christmas but won't practice riding it until two summers later. Mom and Dad really stretched their budget to buy it, but it sits in the garage gathering dust until the hypercautious child feels he's up to riding it.

Or take the Beaver child who won't jump in the deep end of the pool, when her younger sister is splashing around fearlessly. Now don't get me wrong: most Beavers will ride and swim eventually—it just takes them longer to try new things. So in the meantime they build patience in siblings and parents—not a bad byproduct!

WHEN HIGH STANDARDS
BECOME DESTRUCTIVE

As we've said throughout this book, there are no right and wrong personalities—only those we understand and those we don't. And every personality type has its particular strengths and weaknesses. For example, painstaking accuracy are great qualities in a doctor. Now I'm not saying that all M.D.s are purebred Beavers. Lions are great as emergency-room physicians when decisions need to be made in a hurry, and Retrievers and Otters usually have a great bedside manner. But this Otter doesn't want anyone but a Beaver to operate on him!

There are downsides to the Beaver persuasion, however. Because of their intense inbred desire for perfection, Beavers can become immobilized by fear of mistakes or possible criticism of their actions. Part of this pressure occurs because Beavers tend to view their work as a part of themselves. They have poured themselves into creating what they consider a perfect—or near-perfect—project. So when a parent or teacher criticizes their drawing or writing assignment, Beavers internalize it as a criticism of who they are. If they earn five As and one B on their report card, they'll tend to view the entire semester as a failure.

Because they dislike imperfection so much, Beavers can have a difficult time accepting God's grace and forgiveness. Special attention needs to be given to show Beavers just how much God loves them—regardless of their performance. Parents' unconditional love can help convince them about God's amazing grace. "You see, at just the right time, when we were still powerless, Christ died for the ungodly. Very rarely will anyone die for a righteous man, though for a good man someone might possibly dare to die. But God demonstrates his own love for us in this: While we were still sinners, Christ died for us" (Romans 5:6-8).

Though your family may not have been blessed with any strong Beavers, you can still make it a point to stress to your children, "There's nothing you can do to make us love you more or love you less." Beavers and Retrievers need special help in this area; you really can't overemphasize unconditional love.

TEMPERING THE BEAVER TRAIT

As with all four personality types, we need to temper or balance the strengths of one persuasion with the strengths of another. For example, each summer at Kanakuk Kamp we had many team-building activities for the kids. We combined skill-building games with a teamwork emphasis. Just as in Marine boot camp, we had obstacle courses (fit for children, of course) called challenge courses. One of them involved swinging on a long rope suspended from a tree from one wooden platform to another. Sound dangerous? Nah. The platforms are only inches off the ground. But the rule was that if you touched the ground on your way over, your entire group had to start the course again from the beginning. So teammates caught each camper as he swung from one platform over to the other.

One boy whom I'll call Jeb had taken a nasty fall a few days previously and had hurt his back. He was recovering and was fit to do this activity, but he was sore and taking things a bit gingerly. When Jeb tried to swing over to the second platform, his teammates missed him, and he swung back to the original platform. But he was low on momentum, so he didn't make it fully back to the deck. His friend Willy could see that Jeb might have a rough landing on the ground, and out of concern for his friend he leaped off the platform to catch him and prevent certain pain. Willy was a strong Golden Retriever and compassion for his friend was tops on his list.

At that point chaos broke loose. The Beavers on the team jumped all over Willy's case, chiding him for breaking the rules, expecting that there would be no question as to whether they would all be penalized and have to start over. They appeared to ignore Jeb's sore back entirely. The Retrievers countered that this was a special case and that Jeb's safety was more important than losing the competition.

Can you picture the scene? Boys yelling and stomping in the dirt, pointing their fingers, each sure that his viewpoint was the only valid one. It was almost comical. I soon saw that I needed to step in and help resolve this one. I decided that I would affirm Willy's helping Jeb, given the circumstances of his injury and other factors. The entire conflict turned out to be a powerful learning opportunity for the kids. Precision in following rules is fine up to a point, but it's the mature Beaver who knows when to temper that strength with love for people.

THE BEAVER IN US ALL

As we have seen, an off-the-chart Beaver tendency can wreak havoc in a person's life as he or she chases the impossible goal of perfection. But a moderate level of the trait can be helpful, both to the Beaver and to the other personality types.

For example, Suzette's brother, Russ, is an Otter-Lion who has never considered himself to have many organizational skills. "I hate to file," he says with a grin. Yet he has in recent years learned to "sort of file" by making different piles of important papers. When he recently needed to find some important data to apply for a mortgage, he was able to go to the right pile and find the documentation required. We know several other people who amaze their friends and relatives when they can dive into what seems to be an unorganized mess and find just what they were looking for. Their typical explanation? "You may not think I'm organized, but I knew just where to look."

"I'll probably never have typed labels for my file folders, meticulously arranged in twelve file cabinets in my garage," Russ grinned. "But I've learned to organize my chaos to the point that I need to." In addition, the computer has added a challenging and fun order to his otherwise potential calamity.

All the personalities can build their organizational skills, but they tend to see the "why" through their own lenses. If you have a child who needs to be more organized, build his motivation through the lens that *he* sees the world through. Lions, for example, can see the usefulness in organization and can use that as motivation to make themselves more Beaver-like. If being organized helps them reach their goals (remember, they're highly goal-oriented), they'll do it. Golden Retrievers also can see the value in being organized, usually in relational terms. An easy way to motivate a Retriever to accomplish tasks is to explain how he or she is

Beavers at a Glance

Beavers tend to like:
   To take their time and do it right
   Clearly defined tasks
   Assignments that require precision

Beavers tend to fear:
   Deadlines
   Criticism of their work
   Risks (they don't want to chance
   failure)

Beavers are motivated by:
   Recognition and approval of their
   work
   The need to be right

helping you. You might say, "It would really help me out if you emptied the dishwasher," or "If you can fold this load of laundry, then we can get out and have more time together shopping tonight." If a Retriever feels as if she is helping someone, then she is usually very willing to get things done.

MOTIVATING YOUR BEAVER

Make sure you've done your homework before approaching a Beaver. If you are a let's-just-do-it Lion or a shoot-from-the-hip Otter parent and your child is a questioning, critical-thinking Beaver, you may be in for some conflict. Beavers need a lot of proof before they will accept something as valid; they demand reliable sources. Once they see the value of the task or rule that you have proposed, Beavers will usually stay with it until it is accomplished according to their high standards. You rarely have to worry about quality control with a Beaver. But don't forget to give your Beaver child plenty of time to complete a task or chore. (Remember, Beavers like to take their time and do it right.) When faced with deadline pressures, Beavers will often slow down even further.

Because Beavers are task-oriented and love making plans, a Daytimer is a priceless tool when it comes to motivating them. Our friend Susan helps her Beaver daughter, Ashley, map out school projects in her Daytimer. Since Beavers sometimes miss deadlines because they don't have something "just right," Susan helps Ashley create realistic deadlines for herself by breaking a big project into several smaller projects. Large wall calendars are great tools for younger Beavers. They enjoy seeing in black and white how many days they have left to study before Friday's spelling test.

It is important that we understand each animal in our family menagerie, and I hope you've had fun—as well as been challenged—as we've introduced you to the four personality styles. But insight into personality mix is not enough. In the pages that follow, you'll learn more about how to motivate your children to become all that they can be, no matter what animal personality they may resemble. In the next chapter, we'll share thirteen practical ways to help kids mature confidently and effectively.

THINKING IT OVER

1. Consider the following saying: "If you don't have time to do it right the first time, do you have enough time to do it again?" Next, consider its corollary: "Be the job large or small, do it right or not at all." Which family members would heartily subscribe to one of those sayings? In reading through this chapter, have you been able to identify the Beavers in your family?

2. Do you have a child or know anyone who is a diligent worker or is particularly known for his or her high-quality work? How long does it take him to complete a project and get it just right? Does it ever get him into trouble when scheduling is important?

3. If you have a Beaver child, what is his characteristic response to you asking him to hurry up and complete a task? Why do you think this occurs?

4. Why do you think a Beaver does not take criticism well? How could you make your criticism more palatable for your Beaver?

5. In this chapter were you able to see the strengths and weaknesses of the Beaver traits? Who in your family needs to either strengthen or tone down his Beaver tendencies? Do *you* need to do either?

PART THREE

FROM THE WILDS TO THE HOME

CHAPTER SEVEN

Motivating Your Family Zoo

TRAVIS'S SIXTH-GRADE SOCCER TEAM WAS TRAILING 3-2 WITH less than one minute to play when he stole the ball from an opponent and began working it toward the goal. As another opponent charged toward him, Travis kicked the ball to his teammate, Jack, who in his position as a forward could drive the ball into the net and tie the game.

But Jack was out of position, and the ball went hurtling across the grass and out of bounds. I (Jim) closed my eyes, imagining what would come next. As center midfielder, Travis served as an on-field coach. And as a Lion, I knew that when he was under pressure, fur would usually fly. I had seen him chastise his teammates in the past. One time he went so far as to go over to Jack, grab him by the jersey, and drag him back into position. I cringed for Jack, who had just been corrected by the coach at halftime and now had blown a chance to tie the game. I waited for Travis to finish him off verbally.

"It's okay, Jack! Just block the ball when it comes back in!" Travis yelled.

I couldn't believe it. Travis was actually focusing on Jack's feelings and not the game! Lions don't naturally back off. Once they smell blood, their instinct is to go in for the kill. "Be ready, Jack. I'm gonna feed the ball to you as soon as I get it," Travis encouraged. Sure enough, Travis stole the ball, then kicked it to Jack, who in turn drove it into the net to tie the game.

As soon as the game was over, I put my arm around Travis's shoulder and said, "Son, I'm really proud of how you've become more sensitive in the past few months. You had every opportunity to blow Jack away, but you backed off and really felt for him. I know that was difficult."

"Thanks, Dad," Travis responded. "But just between you and me, I did tell him off in my head."

I chuckled to myself, understanding his struggle. I was proud that Travis was learning to temper his Lionish approach and become more sensitive to others.

AFFIRMATIVE ACTION

Affirmation is the key to motivating any personality type. Try to catch your children doing right, and then really brag on them.

For instance, while I was at Kanakuk, one of the things I stressed to the camp staff was that "there are no little losers" at camp. If a kid comes in dead last in an event, but he gave it his best, he receives as many hugs and encouraging words from the staff as the one who came in first. If our focus as parents or teachers is constantly on the negative, we will close off our relationships with our children. It is much better to focus on the positive characteristics they display throughout the day.

I know a school principal who made a list of the school's "losers" each year. These were the kids who were doing poorly academically and socially. He would secretly assign four teachers to each "loser," and let the teachers know areas in which the student needed work or encouragement. These teachers were to make it a point to make contact with that student each day.

"Hey, John, good to see you today. How's it going in biology?"

Initially the kids would just grunt or shrug. But the teachers would tell them, "You can do it. I believe in you."

After just a few weeks, a dramatic change occurred in these students who had felt negative about themselves and their schoolwork. Their grades began to go up, and they became more involved in school activities and with their peer group—all because someone was showing interest and encouraging them.

Another element of affirmation is understanding how perceived personality weaknesses can be transformed into strengths. For instance, a person who is negatively labeled as picky could be positively identified as thorough. When the positive aspect of a trait is affirmed, the negative aspect is less likely to be predominant.

AFFIRMATIVE CORRECTION

Affirming positive behavior does not mean we ignore negative behavior. We simply don't make as big an issue of our children's wrong behavior as we do of their good behavior.

Dr. Bruce Narramore makes an important distinction between punishment and discipline.[1] Punishment focuses on past misbehavior; discipline focuses on future right behavior. Punishment emphasizes how bad the child has been; discipline points out how good the child is and can be. Discipline communicates that we don't want our children's actions to spoil the great future that is in store for them. Remember, we want to motivate our children, not demoralize them.

That is why natural consequences work well for older children. Obviously, we're not suggesting that parents intentionally allow a small child to touch a hot burner. But rather than disciplining a child for taking a bite out of the bathroom soap, allow the horrible taste and stomachache to do the job of disciplining for you. The motivation against further soap nibbling is built in. (We do advocate proper first aid to neutralize the effects.)

In order to motivate future positive behavior, the consequence also needs to fit the crime. In this way time-out, loss of privileges, grounding, and so on teach right behavior.

"If I hit my friend over the head with a dump truck, I won't be able to play with my friend for a while." Not being able to watch TV for three days has no connection with the crime.

"If I pitch a baseball through the neighbor's window, I will have to pay for the repair." Being banned from video games for a week fails to reinforce the rule that the neighbor's house is not to be used as a backstop.

"If I stay out past curfew, I won't be going out for a while." Having to set and clear the table for a week is not a reminder to be in at the appointed hour.

A wise horseman knows to give his animal freedom while still holding onto the reins. The horse knows it is free to make decisions, but if it starts to get into a dangerous area, the rider will gently pull in the reins until the animal is back on the safe path. In the same way, an effective parent holds the reins loosely. Use just enough pressure to guide your child, but not so much that you choke her. Just the right amount of control is the secret to guiding horses—and to rearing healthy Lions, Otters, Retrievers, and Beavers.

THIRTEEN WAYS TO MOTIVATE YOUR KIDS, NATURALLY

What child doesn't want to succeed in life and experience harmony at home? But there are many roadblocks to these goals: personality strengths pushed out of balance to become weaknesses, life skills never learned, coping mechanisms that hurt others. A big part of a parent's job is to help remove those roadblocks. Another part is to do everything possible to motivate our children to grow, learn, and mature.

Here are some tried-and-true methods we and other parents have used to help each animal in our personal zoos flourish.

1. Make your kids' activities a top priority in your schedule. One man I (Jim) know grew up with parents who never attended a practice or performance put on by the high school marching band in which he played. He was an excellent clarinet player, but his parents never came to watch him. A deep wound of rejection formed in his heart and he is still dealing with it today. He has a lovely family and is recovering from the hurts in his heart, but it's not easy.

If your child is participating in sports or drama or choir or whatever, show you care by making time in your schedule. Actions really do speak louder than words. And these days time is more precious than gold. When you make time to attend and applaud, you're giving your child real gold in relational terms. Your presence is a strong nonverbal statement of your support and love.

Take the time to learn about your children's areas of greatest interest. I remember forcing myself to learn about competitive swimming (which I never pursued as a youngster) just because our kids liked it. In fact, I earned certification as a swim official. My life has been enriched because I took time to pursue an area that appealed to my kids. Your life can be enriched, too.

One caution on this use-of-your-time issue. You can go overboard as a parent and never allow yourself time for your own interests. And even though you might do it out of a noble motive, it's unhealthy in the long term for all concerned. Be sure to permit yourself some time, too. This is especially true for full-time mothers, who can burn out from so much contact with their kids. Husbands need to step in regularly and give their wives some time off to themselves. If you're a single mom, recruit dads or single men to roughhouse and do other activities with your boys. Similarly, invite other moms or single women over to spend time with your daughters.

2. Write encouraging notes and hide them where your kids will find them. This may seem corny, but it's a fabulous way to put a spark of encouragement into your child's day. A day at school can seem extremely long, and when your child is reminded that she has people at home who love her, she can gain support and courage to keep going through the tough times.

In the case of preschool children who can't read a card, you can adapt the procedure with a favorite toy, beloved treasure, or stuffed animal. For example, John and Cindy Trent used a little stuffed bear their family named Love Bear. Their preschool daughter Kari was likely to find this little friend in the bathroom drawer when she went to brush her teeth. John says it was a joy to see her "light up like a Christmas tree" when she found their hidden love gift.

Hiding encouraging notes or treasures can work in reverse, too. John chuckles as he recalls how Kari would return the favor. "I found little Love Bear in my shoe and in the pocket of my robe. And Cindy even found it in the refrigerator!" Such family fun can go a long way toward strengthening vital relationships.

3. When correcting, use a "praise sandwich." Surround correcting words with affirmative words: praise-correct-praise. Suzette and I have reaped the benefits of the "praise sandwich" concept as we've tried to help Jill grow in her weakest area: organization. You've learned that Otters are not detail-oriented; neither do they plan very far into the future. If you have an Otter, homework can be a frustrating and tiring experience. There can be great trauma as bedtime nears and his or her assignments are not yet completed.

When she was in grade school, we would allow Jill to

begin her homework assignments on her own, as she should. But she knew to begin early enough in the afternoon or evening to allow for play time before bed. When she reached an impasse on a particular assignment, she would call on her mom or me for assistance. Knowing that the problem was usually misunderstanding the instructions (most Otters are guilty of this, including yours truly), we would first look at the work she had already completed and praise her for that. Then we would go over the instructions once again. We helped her with one or two problems or exercises and made sure she understood the procedure. Then we gently underlined the original difficulty: not paying close attention to the instructions. We completed the time with praise for how she picked up the correct procedure, did some problems on her own, and was making great strides toward completing her homework in time for some play before bed.

4. Listen to your kids. Listen actively to what your kids have to say as if it were the most important thing you could be doing at the moment. Listening is probably the most important thing you *can* do. When you consider what's more important— knocking off that day's to-do list or affirming your child—you'll start having a happier home.

5. Guide your kids in setting realistic goals, then help them implement a plan to accomplish them. Remember, kids are people, too. And they like to plan and carry out their plans just as Mom and Dad do. But sometimes life can be a bit scary for a little person, so they need you to hold their hand as a guide and cheerleader.

6. Help your kids see a positive—but realistic—future.[2] Sometimes life can seem overwhelming to a youngster, so we need to provide a hopeful look to the future, based on the child's strengths. If we can color his or her world with such thinking, motivation is bound to bloom.

We say "realistic" because unbounded optimism can lead to disillusionment if the view toward the future is unrealistic. In other words, if you allow your child to assume he's going to land a Rhodes Scholarship when he's ready for college, you may be setting him up for disappointment. It is better to challenge him to consider carefully what major he's going to pursue. Then let the particular college be chosen later, when it's time to make that decision.

The wisdom here is not to let every kid who can shoot a basketball through the hoop plan his life around the certainty that he'll land Michael Jordan's job when he grows up. He had better plan on getting a good education and working a normal job, rather than having "To Star in the NBA" on his resumé under "Employment Objective." As parents who've experienced life, we need to bring our maturity to bear on our child's view of the future, making sure he is thinking realistically. Not that we need to be pessimistic! It's just a matter of balancing unbridled optimism and cautious realism.

7. Allow your kids to excel without the pressure of living up to your past successes—or your desired successes for them. Don't fall into the trap of living your life through your kids. They are unique individuals and don't deserve to become entangled in your unfulfilled hopes and expectations. The classic illustration of this, of course, is when the overbearing parent explodes on the sideline of the football game and rips the coach's head off "because Johnny didn't get enough playing time."

Once we've gotten our focus off our own needs and wants and start working for the best interest of our child, considering his or her own unique makeup (both strengths and weaknesses), we'll be a long way down the road to family and parenting success. True love is working for the best of one another. And nowhere but in the family do we have more opportunity to experience this.

8. Place emphasis on the effort your kids put forth in any activity rather than on their success or failure. Realize that your children can't win at everything every single time. In every competition there has to be a winner and a loser. Your task is to make your kids feel like winners no matter what the outcome. Encourage them to give any task their best effort and to feel good about that.

When the counselors at Kanakuk celebrated every child's achievement, whether he was the first one across the finish line or the last, it became contagious. The other kids learned to hug and give high fives to the last one across the line, too. Excellence is always a worthwhile goal, but that should be measured by the child's effort, not the final results of a task or competition.

9. Allow your kids time and space to be kids. Too much scheduled activity can cause burnout and even illness. Likewise, too high an expectation level can cause resentment. Sometimes we start treating our kids like little adults, and that can cause serious problems later in life.

When our kids were thirteen, eleven, and seven, the local TV station in Springfield, Missouri, wanted to do a special news report titled "Yuppies Pushing Their Kids to Be Superachievers." They came out to our home and shot their video. I sure hope they weren't disappointed. First off, we're hardly yuppies. And although our kids do tend to be high achievers, we don't put undue pressure on them to perform.

As Suzette said on the TV newscast (regarding Jill's working out with her swim team three afternoons per week), "If one of our kids wants to stop an activity, they're free to do so. We let them choose the level of commitment they want to make." Again, it's a matter of balancing your level of expectations with what's appropriate for your child's age level. It's fine to encourage your kids to excel, but not if your family ends up a charred ember in the burnout bonfire.

10. Help your kids cultivate special skills in which they wish to excel. In other words, play to their strengths. For example, if you have a naturally active and agile child, you might choose to encourage her in sports rather than chess. Conversely, if you have a studious, reading-oriented child, you might encourage him in academic pursuits over, say, mountain climbing.

But don't get us wrong—parents need to encourage balance in their children's lives. Bookworms need to get outdoors regularly, and wiggleworms need to study history. But keep in mind that you're doing your children a big favor if you can recognize their strengths and then provide settings to help them excel in those areas.

Variety, as the saying goes, is the spice of life. Applied here, that means we need to expose our kids to new areas of activity on occasion. Let them try out a new activity before you "lock them in." For example, rent downhill skis and pay for a round of lessons to see if it "fits" before investing in an expensive ski equipment package.

11. Consider how you can enhance a current activity before "switching horses." When you suspect your child no longer feels challenged by an activity, provide a means to take her to a more advanced skill level instead of dropping the activity altogether. This could include signing up for an advanced class, a tougher sports league, a summer camp tailored to that activity, a more advanced piano teacher, and so on. In this way you take advantage of the experience your child has in the field, and he doesn't have to start at square one in a new area of endeavor.

Sometimes this strategy can lead to a real breakthrough and can catapult a child into a superior level of performance. This is especially true of children with Lion characteristics. Travis thrives on challenge. When he was younger, his interest in soccer began to wane as he acquired a higher skill level while competing in intramurals. Rather than drop the sport altogether, however, we discovered club soccer. This more advanced level of competition renewed the challenge Travis needed to further sharpen his skills.

12. Empathize with your kids' failures. If your child feels he has failed in an activity, empathize with him by sharing about one of the failures you have experienced—and survived. Kids tend to think their parents always succeed in everything they do, so sharing our childhood failures can help them feel okay when they try something and don't get it perfect the first time.

One night a friend of ours shared with his daughters how he had succumbed to peer pressure as a youngster and got in trouble for shoplifting. Since then, they've frequently asked their dad to retell the story.

"I think I was about ten years old, and my friend dared me to go steal some candy with him at a convenience store," he recalls with a wry smile. "I knew it was wrong and teetered on the edge of decision, but in the end I wanted to impress my buddy, so I agreed to do it." (Our friend is strong on the Otter scale which can predispose him to follow such plans put forth by others.)

"When the shopkeeper caught us loitering about the candy section and then trying to slip out unnoticed, he nabbed us. Just to teach us a lesson we'd never forget, he called the sheriff, who took us home to our parents.

"I'll never forget the shame I felt when my parents opened the front door and there I stood with the law at my side. That really taught me an important lesson about right and wrong." He uses that story primarily to teach his kids about the dangers of peer pressure.

As a parent you have a wealth of experiences in life to draw upon to teach and encourage your kids. And you should take advantage of those resources. Kids have memories like elephants when it comes to your childhood experiences, so tell your kids what it was like for you to have been a kid once. That will help them when being a kid gets tough for them.

13. If all else fails, simply ask, "How can I help?" Every parent wants to have the perfect solution for every crisis, but sometimes that's just not possible. We encourage parents to keep in their hip pocket a one-size-fits-all solution for those moments when a plan doesn't leap into their heads: Simply ask your child, "How can I help?" Often children know exactly what they need, even better than their parents do.

We have done this several times with each one of our kids, which demonstrates to them their high value to us. A few years ago we were in Canton, Ohio, for the NCAA Swimming and Diving Championships. Jason had won the fifty-yard freestyle event the year before, shocking everyone by his success as a freshman. His teammates, coaches, and even Jason himself had high expectations for the NCAA race, so everyone was shocked again when he finished a disappointing fifth place with a slower time than he'd swum the year before. He was still All-American and one of the top swimmers in the country, but he felt he'd let his team down.

I (Jim) didn't know what to say after the race, and there was nothing in the world that I could do. So I hugged Jason and asked, "How can I help?" My son grinned and answered simply, "Your just being here is all the help I need." Who would have known?

⑤

In the next chapter we'll examine a real application of this material: Just how do parents cope with a family made up of different-aged kids? For example, when you have teenagers in the same menagerie as preschoolers, you have to do some fancy gear shifting. We'll look at how to adapt your parenting style to make the connection with kids in each age group.

THINKING IT OVER

1. What are some unusual and surprising ways you can praise and encourage your children (for example, notes in a lunch box, flowers, or balloons)?
2. How much time per week do you spend at your kids' activities? Do you think this is adequate? Do they?
3. What do you do to reinforce and encourage your child after a disappointing defeat or a poor performance? What method would most fit his or her personality mix?
4. Are there any areas of control that you are holding onto intensely? How could you loosen the reins without dropping them? (If you draw a blank on this one, try asking friends for suggestions.)
5. In contrast to grasping the reins too tightly, are there any areas in your family in which there is a total lack of control? What can you do to get a grip on the situation? (Again, if you have difficulty strategizing, consult friends who seem to have this area balanced.)

Notes
1. Bruce Narramore, *Help! I'm a Parent* (Grand Rapids: Zondervan, 1972).
2. This is adapted from one of the central themes of *The Blessing*, by Gary Smalley and John Trent (Nashville: Thomas Nelson, 1986), pp. 81-96.

CHAPTER EIGHT

Appreciating Age-Level Differences

THE BRAWNER FAMILY ZOO DOESN'T VISIT MALLS. IT PROWLS THEM. Like hungry carnivores, our children stalked these modern hunting grounds for new quarry.

One day's game was feeding on quarters in the darkness of the video arcade. Jason and Travis had come well-armed with pockets full of ammunition to track it down and defeat it.

"Daaaaaaaad!" Jill howled as her brothers hurried off down the walkway. "Why can't I go, too?"

I held tightly to her hand as our seven-year-old struggled to get free and race after her brothers.

"You're too young, Jill," I tried to explain.

"I am not! I can reach where you put the money in, and I can reach the joystick," she argued.

"I know you're old enough to play the games, but you're not responsible enough to go to the arcade by yourself."

Jill stopped tugging on my weary arm and looked puzzled.

I explained that being responsible included turning off the light in her room when she leaves or feeding our dog— all without being asked.

"Oh."

That was the end of our discussion, but we were delighted when Jill began turning off her light and feeding the dog. She not only accomplished these chores, but she also took on some additional ones without being asked. Several months later, she was enjoying our small town mall with her brothers.

One of the many challenges of taming the family zoo is

using the appropriate direction and discipline at different stages of our critters' development. Obviously, we related to our sixteen-year-old differently from our ten-year-old.

Let's look at the various personality types as they are cross-referenced with three phases of development. For ease of reference, we'll divide childhood into three age brackets: preschool (from birth to age five), school age (age five to twelve), and teenagers (age thirteen to eighteen). We'll look briefly at the various unique conditions of each age bracket, then look at how the four personalities express themselves during each phase.

UNDERSTANDING THE PRESCHOOLER

Preschoolers' attention spans are roughly one minute for each year of age. Some parents may question if it's even that long. These are what some have called the "make it or break it" years. Research and experience tell us that the bulk of a child's values, outlook on life (what's trustworthy, what's frightening), and even vocabulary is established in large measure by age six.

Their basic spiritual values are also well established. At this age, children are able to understand what pleases God, that the Bible is God's Book, and that the church is His house. Preschoolers perceive God as a real and loving Person and can begin to pray intelligently.

The young child's thinking is concrete rather than conceptual, so he learns best through his five senses. He is generally at the first stage in moral development: discipline and obedience orientation.[1] This stage is summed up best by "If it feels good, do it. If it doesn't, don't." The child thinks, *Willfully throwing my full bowl of cereal on the floor is followed by appropriate consequences. Cross off throwing full bowls of cereal on the floor as a feel-good activity. On the other hand, if I manage to get half a spoon of cereal in the near vicinity of my mouth, I get an ecstatic hug and praise from Mom and Dad. I'll do that again.*

One of the important lessons that can be learned during this stage is sharing. Kris Cooper, a camp director, uses the buddy system with his own children. All members of the family are our buddies. When siblings want to play with the same toy at the same time, Kris says, "We're all buddies. So it's okay to let our buddy play with 'our' toy for a while."

Kris prefers this method to saying, "Okay, you play with it for five minutes, then let your brother play with it for five minutes." The buddy system emphasizes affection and loyalty, things the simple time-sharing system lacks.

Lion Preschoolers

As you might expect, little Lions are just big Lions in miniature. They are the go-getters in a group of youngsters. They're first in line, first to answer a question or riddle, and even first to plop their mat down at preschool when it's nap time.

Lion cubs tend to have many questions for Mom or Dad, which can sometimes get tiresome, as any parent knows. But be careful not to interpret a young Lion's questions, which often challenge the authority structure and the status quo, as blatant rebellion. Lions are not necessarily challenging you as a parent; they may just be stretching their tails. If they learn to temper their strength of will at the appropriate time, they can grow up to be influential leaders.

In the early years, though, you do need to be aware that sometimes your cub will challenge your authority as a parent. That's when you need to become firm as the person in charge. After all, no matter how cute that little Lion or Lioness may be, he or she is still quite capable of willful defiance. If you're a parent with a strong Golden Retriever trait and a very weak Lion trait, beware of one of your Lion kids controlling you. It might sound ridiculous, but it can happen. The Retriever parent must be especially firm when it comes to enforcing rules with their Lion kids. In parenting it's generally true that success is a matter of balancing love and limits. With Lion kids this is especially true.

Otter Preschoolers

Perhaps the most important lesson that preschool Otters need to learn is the importance of orderliness. Left to themselves, Otter children will feel just fine about always having a bedroom that, as the classic line from mothers goes, "looks like a cyclone hit it."

Marsha and Richard Beach were blessed with two daughters who cover the opposite ends of the spectrum in this regard. Whitney has a highly developed Beaver sense, whereas Stacey is almost pure Otter. When these two girls were young, they shared a room, and a small one at that. There was plenty of opportunity for friction when Whitney kept her part of the room neat as a pin, and then Mom asked them both to clean up their room. Sound familiar? When differing personality types have to live in close proximity to each other, sparks can fly. Yet it provides an opportunity to learn balanced living.

Marsha decided to let consequences teach Stacey the importance of cleaning up after herself. She set the rule that both girls had to clean their room, make their bed, and get dressed before breakfast each morning. Failure to comply with this standard resulted in losing TV privileges after school so the child would have time to clean her half of the room.

As you might guess, high Beaver Whitney had little trouble with such a rule, while high Otter Stacey had plenty. But eventually Stacey got the message, and one day Marsha nearly fell over when she walked into the girls' room and found Stacey dressed with her hair brushed, making her bed. And, best of all, Marsha was walking on the floor. (Normally she was walking on the clothes Stacey had strewn about the night before!) When Marsha let out a gasp of pleasant surprise, Stacey said, "Mom, I've decided that I'm not going to have a messy room anymore. I want to watch cartoons in the afternoon." Marsha and Richard poured on the praise over the next few weeks to reinforce Stacey's decision.

We can learn a couple of things from the Beaches' experience. One, constant moaning and groaning from parents has little effect—especially when the behavior simply reflects the child's basic personality type. Instead of ruining your relationship with your child by constantly nagging and complaining, use consequences. Two, customize the consequences to your child's personality mix. For a high Otter like Stacey, whose primary motivator is to have fun, the loss of a visually fun activity such as watching cartoons was significant. For other strong Otters, restriction of time with their peers can also motivate since they are such social creatures.

Remember to reinforce positive behavior once it comes. Everybody likes to feel successful, and you can't overdo praise.

Retriever Preschoolers

One of the unique qualities of Golden Retrievers is their sensitivity to others. But in the little pup this can manifest itself in oversensitivity. If you're a Lion-type parent, you need to be especially careful in dealing with a Retriever child.

Golden Retrievers can read nonverbal signals from Mom and Dad like a book. I (Jim) remember when Jason was young, he referred to "that look" as all the motivation he needed from Dad to reform. In general, you don't need to discipline Golden Retrievers as much as other personality types because they'll "get it" much more easily. Be careful, though, about sending too many negative nonverbal signals, or you could crush your pup's spirit. Nonverbal signals can also be positive. A smile, a pat on the back, a hug, or an attentive ear can build a great relationship. Balance is the key.

Beaver Preschoolers

As we have learned, Beavers are prone to the affliction of perfectionism. And it's in the preschool stage that perfectionism can either be encouraged or extinguished.

Beaver youngsters will take enormous time and care to, say, color precisely within the lines of their coloring book. And if they stray outside the lines, watch out! They'll quickly tear up the picture or crunch it into the smallest ball imaginable. Be careful to communicate to a high Beaver child that his or her acceptability is not based on performance. Do everything you can to teach your little Beaver that while high standards are great, perfection is not the goal. If left unchecked, such behavior can lead to a lifetime of misery.

UNDERSTANDING SCHOOL-AGE CHILDREN

As children mature, they become more aware that right behavior is more than simply what feels good at the moment. They begin to develop a concept of the rightness and wrongness of an action, and social pressure to follow the rules begins to develop. They begin to play cooperatively, as opposed to playing alone while with other children. Though they are still essentially self-centered, they are growing in friendliness and in their desire to please other children and adults. This is where peer pressure begins to get a foothold. Make sure to keep communication lines open during this important period (indeed throughout the parenting years).

This is a crucial stage in the child's spiritual life. Older children can sincerely worship, obey, and trust God, as well as learn basic doctrines. From grades five to nine, children are most likely to make a decision to follow or reject Christ.

At this stage children can learn through natural consequences, as we discussed in chapter 3. Remember, we need to allow our children to fail occasionally, rather than always bailing them out. By learning a valuable lesson through failure, children learn to "fail forward," making progress even through their mistakes.

School-Age Lions

Lion cubs by this age have a few of their teeth in, and it generally shows. In other words, they have an emerging leadership style that must be managed.

To illustrate, Travis entered second grade under a first-year teacher, Miss Duke. At the time, I (Jim) was the principal at the middle school on the same property. Miss Duke was a well-liked teacher, but she had the first-year jitters. She was just a bit unsure of herself, and gave directions to the class in a hesitant manner.

Lions are so accustomed to being in charge and having others obey them that it often bugs them when others don't "hop to" right away—even when they're not the ones in charge! So it was with Travis, even at the tender age of seven. Whenever he sensed that the students weren't obeying with sufficient promptness, he would bark out, "Hurry up!" or "Get in line!" or "You kids—sit down!" He wanted them to have proper respect for the authority figure, Miss Duke.

But Travis's behavior was dangerous in one respect: if he did it in an angry tone of voice, his classmates would resent him and not be his friends. So he had to learn to direct them in a helpful, friendly way rather than in an offensive, divisive way. And he had to let Miss Duke learn to buck up and take charge. Most first-year teachers wind up learning this valuable lesson.

School-Age Otters

Otter children in the elementary school years usually are having lots of fun doing what adults call networking. In other words, they are having a blast with so many new friends. They seek to have contact with the maximum number of little chums possible, and this can occasionally get out of hand.

One time Jill wanted to have a sleep-over for her birthday. We asked her to come up with a guest list, and she did: twenty-three friends were on that list. After I (Suzette) picked myself up off the floor at the prospect of two dozen giggling girls in the house, we discussed some more realistic goals, and I engaged Jill in planning the details.

Another area of need for Otter children is effective communication. Once Jill brought home an assignment from her fourth-grade teacher, Mrs. Frazier. The students were supposed to replace what the teacher called tired words such as "stuff," "things," "good," and "bad" with more specific words or phrases. At this age it is important to teach our children how to express themselves effectively. Otter children, without knowing or even realizing it, may ramble on and on. We found that asking Jill to explain a statement or word—even if we knew what she meant—taught her to be more thoughtful with her words.

School-Age Retrievers

The beauty of Golden Retrievers at this stage of life is that they can "put feet" to their feelings of empathy and consideration for others. They can excel at doing deeds of kindness for others, and parents need to applaud that and let it rub off on the other members of the family.

Nine-year-old Jason showed us his capabilities in this area when his brother Travis injured himself in a biking accident. Due to Travis's complete and total lack of fear, which is common in Lions, he earned the early nickname "an accident waiting to happen." Do you have a child like that?

We lived on the crest of a hill at that time, and seven-year-old Travis loved to race down the hill on his bike and, just at the right moment, do an airborne Evil Knievel leap. What happened one day still makes us shudder. Our daredevil pushed his bicycle to the max and leaped into the air with unusual speed. Unfortunately, he got off to a crooked start. While airborne, he crashed into the pillar that separated our two-car garage. Jason yelled for Mom to come to the rescue, and she rushed Travis to the hospital to get stitches in his chin.

Throughout the ordeal, sensitive Jason experienced tremendous empathy with his fallen comrade brother. While we were at the hospital, he decorated Travis's twisted bike with a sign saying "Welcome Home" and tied streamers and candy on it. That sight really gave Travis a lift after a traumatic afternoon.

While Retrievers are delightful at this age, parents need to be aware that problems can develop later on if these pups are not taught healthy boundaries. Because Retrievers tend to be people pleasers, they can be taken advantage of and can forget to take care of their own needs. While your Retriever is young, affirm his people-loving tendency while encouraging him to love and care for himself as well.

School-Age Beavers

During their early school years young Beavers will earn decent grades. In fact, they are often straight-A students, given their predisposition for excellence. When there's a list to memorize, they nail it down 100 percent; when there's a procedure to learn, they're usually first to understand it thoroughly. They can often be used by the teacher as examples of "how to do it right."

As good as this sounds, however, it can get out of hand if Beaver kids get their strokes exclusively from performance, such as getting good grades. Parents need to make sure to affirm them in settings other than those in which they perform well. Otherwise they will grow up with a performance-based mindset and an overdeveloped sensitivity to criticism.

Some friends told us of their first parent-teacher conference during their Beaver son's first year in school. The teacher started out on a positive note: "Your son does exceptional work," she said slowly. Our friends beamed. Little Johnny always cared for all the details in his chores at home, too. They were so proud of such a fine report.

But then the teacher shared the rest of the story. Our friends' faces fell when the teacher explained, "The only problem is, I never see much of his work. He's always working on it to make it better and hardly ever turns it in."

Since no one can be perfect, our Beaver children will be setting themselves up for disappointment if we allow them to navigate through life with a perfectionistic orientation.

UNDERSTANDING TEENAGERS

A teen's brain is hungering for new information. Adolescents are able to deal with some abstract thinking and symbolism, and their sense of humor is developing (as well as their capacity for daydreaming).

During their teen years, kids are also developing what Lawrence Kohlberg calls "the social contract" and the notion of "universal ethics."[2] Social contracts are codes or agreements of behavior. Thus teens respond well to what we call contracting.

Contracting is an exercise in give-and-take as parent and child work out an agreement for such things as curfews or other privileges. For instance, like most sixteen-year-olds, Jason wanted a car. We worked out a detailed contract that listed privileges and corresponding responsibilities.

"As you know, son, with privileges come responsibilities. And the more responsibility you show, the more privileges you will be allowed," I (Jim) began. Jason nodded his head, and I continued.

"The first responsibility you need to show before we get you a car is changing the oil. I'll show you how it's done, but then I want you to be regularly checking the oil in the family car. If it gets low, it's your responsibility to add oil.

"This first three months, we also want you to keep a record of the car's expenses such as gas, oil, license, insurance, repairs, and so on." I wanted Jason to realize the cost of owning a car.

We also established some consequences if Jason didn't fulfill his responsibility. For instance, he was financially responsible for any speeding tickets and any corresponding increase in our insurance.

Another way contracting can work is in helping a teen break a bad habit. Most habits take at least three weeks to take root—and often even longer to break—so don't overreact when you see inappropriate behavior. It may simply be a bad habit rather than your child being irreversibly evil. And as a bad habit is learned, it can be unlearned over time. So, contract for him or her to eliminate the habit totally in twenty-one days, the minimum time to learn or unlearn a habit.

Say, for instance, your teen is using crude language. A contract could allow three slip-ups the first week, two the second, and only one the third. Establish consequences for each crude word over the weekly limit. As we emphasized elsewhere, make sure the punishment fits the crime. We've found this tapering off method much more effective than trying to force a child to give up a habit cold turkey.

We've had both written and unwritten contracts with our kids. Because we want to make sure each contract is clearly understood, we've asked our children to restate what we've just agreed to. For instance, Jason and some friends wanted to ride their bikes to the hospital to visit Travis when he was laid up with pneumonia. We had seen how some of his friends rode bikes: no helmets, no hands, and no direct route. Somehow these boys took shortcuts that always wound up at the mall.

We gave Jason specific instructions, and then asked him to repeat them. (Teens have so many changes going on in their lives that it's rare they hear everything parents say.) Jason sighed, then repeated, "Right, Dad. Wear my helmet. Keep both hands on the handlebars. Don't take a detour to the mall. Be home by six o'clock."

Practicing communication and being consistent with regulations is important with a rapidly maturing young person. In this way, both parties know the terms of the contract exactly, and both are more often pleased with the results.

Lion Teens

Lion children can thrive in the teen years, since they enjoy a lot of activity and challenges. The numerous offerings of school and church in terms of extracurricular activities — clubs, sports, service opportunities, and so on — make a hearty meal for Lion teens. They are becoming adults little by little, and because they don't have to work fulltime beyond their schoolwork, these years can be a paradise to the well-directed teenage cub.

But therein lies the rub. If parents don't guide young Lions and Lionesses into healthy activities, they may end up in unhealthy ones. They are typically fireballs of energy during this stage of life, and you will probably be challenged to keep up with them. Don't be afraid to set ambitious goals with them. Remember, it's difficult to overchallenge a true Lion. Try to funnel their energies into areas where they can do well, and you will minimize the mischief that an idle Lion is prone to.

Otter Teens

Otter teenagers are often known as the class clowns, due to their frequent comical remarks made at opportune moments. Or should we say inopportune? Often an Otter, in his desire to be liked by his classmates, opens his mouth only to put his foot in it. He might think his quick remark was funny, but sometimes it can cross the bounds of kindness and hurt others' feelings.

Otters need guidance from parents and teachers to learn when and when not to cut up. Help them see that there is an appropriate time to be serious and an appropriate time to be lighthearted. "There is a time for everything, and a season for every activity under heaven . . . a time to weep and a time to laugh, a time to mourn and a time to dance" (Ecclesiastes 3:1,4).

Consequences can teach them a lesson as well. When I (Jim) was in high school I learned the hard way that there is a time for everything. I couldn't resist the impulse as I drew back on a rather large rubber band that was aimed at the principal's backside. With highly skilled accuracy, my elastic missile found its mark.

What I in my immaturity thought was cute turned out to be a long and painful walk to his office. I was terrified—not so much at the threat of the shameful three-day suspension from school, but from what I might get from my dad when I got home. Needless to say, I learned my lesson. Otters sometimes need to learn the hard way.

Retriever Teens

If by chance you have a Golden Retriever firstborn in your tribe, followed by the other temperaments, you probably got spoiled with that child and have wondered ever since what happened to the rest of them. Retrievers are good listeners and good friends. You may have to "jump start" them on a project, but once they begin they do just fine.

It's important that you have a close relationship with your Retriever teen. This has a dual purpose. First, Retrievers need an outlet to vent their feelings because they hurt deeply when others let them down. They rarely let others down. Second, it will allow you to have input when they face peer pressure, a seduction to which they are particularly prone.

One mother said in exasperation, "My son Karl never talks to me! If I don't ask the right questions, I'll never hear what he's thinking." She was right in that Golden Retrievers aren't as talkative as, say, Otters. And in the face of interacting with a Lion, Retrievers tend to lay low. Parents need to resist the temptation to discourage this natural quietness and simply value the child's temperament while actively seeking communion with their pup.

Beaver Teens

The teen Beaver has little patience with others who don't measure up to his high standards. And Beavers often turn on themselves as well. The teenage Beaver can, as the saying goes, be his own worst enemy, and sometimes he can develop a poor-me attitude that borders on depression. As parents we need to recognize this propensity for what it is and counter it with a more realistic attitude than holding oneself to a standard of perfection.

Most important, teen Beavers need much TLC. Plenty of unconditional love can help tremendously as they learn to live with their human limitations. Beavers need to be told often that they are valuable for who they are, not just for what they do. You can never go overboard on affirming their inherent worth. Remind them regularly that no matter how well or how poorly they perform in any area of life, you will always love them.

If left unchecked, out-of-control perfectionistic attitudes can harden into a permanent way of looking at life. Remember, your teenager is almost an adult, so if he is expressing out-of-balance Beaver traits, help him achieve a balance.

⊚

For many people, the most mystifying aspect of interpersonal relationships comes in truly understanding the opposite sex. Whether it's parent-to-parent or parent-to-child, getting a grasp on gender differences can be a tremendous help in improving family relationships. We'll look at this aspect in the next chapter.

THINKING IT OVER

1. At what age did you begin to grant increasing privileges to your children? Did any one child seem to be more responsible than another? Why? Can you see personality mix coming into play in this area?

2. If you have more than one child, how do you differentiate privileges from one child to the next? Is this fair for all concerned?

3. Have you ever caught yourself praising your children solely for their performances to the neglect of expressing unconditional love? Have you ever praised them for just being your children?

4. What methods of discipline do you find most effective at each age level? Do you think you should make some adjustments to your disciplinary style after reading this chapter? Why or why not?

5. Ask your spouse or a friend to rate your relationship

with each child on a scale of one to ten (ten being best). When you tuck your child into bed (for older children you may choose another setting), ask her where she would rank your relationship using the same scale.

Notes

1. Lawrence Kohlberg, "Development of Moral Character and Moral Ideology," in M. L. Hoffman and W. Hoffman, *Review of Child Development: Volume 1* (New York: Russell Sage Foundation, 1964), pp. 383-431.
2. Kohlberg, pp. 383-431.

CHAPTER NINE

Celebrating Male/Female Differences

THE DIFFERENCES BETWEEN MALES AND FEMALES ARE FASCINATING. I (Suzette) was intrigued to watch this come to light with Tom, a family friend, who attended one of Jill's volleyball games with us. Halfway through the first game Branson was down 8-0. Our girls couldn't seem to do anything right. We missed easy hits, the serves seemed to land just outside the line, and no one seemed to be hustling on the defense. Coach called a time out. Tom turned to me and said, "Suzette, why do girls do that?"

"Do what?" I answered.

"Have you noticed that every time someone misses a hit or goofs up, the other five girls on the floor go to her, pat her, and tell her it's okay? It's not okay! They need to get with the program! Can you imagine guys patting each other and saying 'That's okay'?"

I laughed and agreed.

Later in the fall we were at the state semi-final play-off football game. Branson was playing a tough team from California, Missouri. California was down by a touchdown. They had the ball in Branson territory and were driving for a certain touchdown. All of a sudden the California running back had the football stripped from his hands as he was tackled. The humiliation of the fumble was enough to make the crowd groan. As he left the field, head down, disgusted, and feeling sorry for himself, one of his team mates slapped him on the helmet and yelled something at him. Something tells me he didn't say, "It's okay."

Some of these differences are culturally learned, but

many are innate. Of course I could write an entire book on figuring out which is which and still not find the whole truth. For now let's briefly cover some of the basic differences and look at factors that will help us be better parents to our coed zoo.

As any parent with children of both genders observes, girls tend to be talkers, squealers, and screamers, while boys like to run, jump, and throw balls through windows. (Of course there are plenty of exceptions, but think about your general observations.) My (Jim's) brother Jerry, father of three girls and no boys says, "Having grown up with two brothers and only one sister, it was a real shock to find my three daughters screaming at the drop of a hat. It drove me crazy for a while, but I got accustomed to it."

Also, girls tend to emphasize relationships, whereas boys emphasize action and power in their play. One girl who baby-sits said, "Boys and girls may both play with cars, but the boys are content to make 'vroom' noises, while the girls pretend they are each driving a car, discussing where they'll go and who they'll visit."

And one father who has both boys and girls marvels, "You know, I never had to teach my two sons how to make all those good boy noises—Bang! Vroom! Aaugh!—they just started making them one day."

On a family vacation to Colorado to ski, we noticed the male/female difference right away. Contrary to what you would predict on a straight personality-type basis, our sons acted a certain way and our daughter acted another. Jason and Travis couldn't wait to get to the top of the mountain and zoom down, hitting the highest jumps and going as fast as they could. Travis nearly killed himself when he went whizzing off a small jump and took off crooked. Thankfully that tree wasn't one foot farther to the right! And Jason, normally laid-back, lacked no gusto.

In contrast, Jill and Suzette skied slowly down the mountain, enjoying the scenery rather than auditioning for the "agony of defeat" segment of "Wild World of Sports" like the guys. Jill wasn't afraid to try more difficult slopes, but enjoyed spending time relating with her mom. Mother and daughter even took time off the slopes to go shopping in the trendy mountain boutiques. (They thought skiing was much more fun if you looked sharp.)

LEARNED DIFFERENCES VS. BIOLOGICAL DIFFERENCES

Back when June and Ward Cleaver were raising the Beaver, society provided clear sex role distinctions: Dad brought home the bacon, and Mom fried it. Women wore dresses; men "wore the pants in the family." Real men were strong and rugged; women were the soft, "weaker sex." Boys were made of frogs and snails and puppy-dog tails; girls were a blend of sugar, spice, and everything nice.

But all these artificial distinctions began to crumble when "Rosie the Riveter" went to work in factories to support the men who had left to fight in World War II. After the peace treaty was signed, many women continued in the work force. At this same time, the modern women's movement began pushing for equality—not only in the workplace but in our culture as a whole. The more radical women of the movement declared that the sexes were "identical from the neck up," and anyone who disagreed was a male chauvinist pig who wanted to keep women in submission by continuing the culture's sexual stereotypes.

If parents have both a boy and girl, however, they soon realize there are bigger differences than just what is physically obvious. But which differences are biological, and which are culturally learned? Biologists and other scientists have discovered that there is an inborn difference between males and females — from the neck up as well as down. And although comprehensive research has not been completed in the entire field, some preliminary results are worth noting.

PHYSICAL DIFFERENCES

There are significant physical distinctions between males and females in addition to what the charts in sex education classes make clear. The following differences are observed in more than three-fourths of the adult men and women examined.[1]

An adult man pumps about 88 percent more blood through his veins than the average woman. In addition, drop for drop females have about 20 percent fewer red blood cells than men. This means that men have a greater capacity for oxygen, and thus energy and endurance.

Men's bodies tend to be 40 percent muscle and 15 percent fat; women tend to be 20 percent muscle and 20 percent fat. Add to this the fact that men's bones tend to be heavier and larger than women's. Most men can out-lift, out-throw, and out-run most women.

But despite a man's apparent physical edge, a woman will outlive the average man by eight years. Women also age more slowly — even without Oil of Olay! Men age approximately 10 percent every ten years after forty years of age. Women age five times slower at a consistent 2 percent each year after child-bearing years. The brains of men also deteriorate more rapidly than those of women.

Although chromosomes determine the sex of a baby at the split second of conception, at twelve weeks of gestation a male and female fetus look identical. At that point a normal male fetus will begin producing androgen, which causes an amazing metamorphosis to a distinctive male body.

The higher level of androgen also tends to make boys more active. A study at Johns Hopkins revealed, however, that girls who were labeled tomboys had higher levels of androgen than other girls. Further proof came from UCLA where researchers discovered that women who took male hormones to prevent miscarriage gave birth to girls who thought and fought more like boys.

At the sixteenth week of a male's fetal development, an even more amazing transformation takes place. At this time, many of the nerve connections between the two hemispheres (sides) of the brain begin to dissolve due to a surge of androgen. Because of this, about 80 percent of males can use only one side of their brain at one time. Most females, however, can retrieve and store information on both sides simultaneously.

Research on stroke victims has revealed that men and women's brains are physically different, too. Because men can't process data in both sides of their brains, a stroke tends to be more debilitating to a man than to a woman. Put in computer terms, in a stroke a disk sector of his brain has been damaged, and he has no backup. The data is forever erased.

Child psychologists at the Gesell Institute for Child Development in New Haven, Connecticut, studied at length the behavior of identical boy and girl twins.[2] They videotaped the children's play and tried to filter out all the cultural factors that could possibly influence behavior. Although they could not totally rule out learned behavior, they found that boys would typically resolve their conflicts with playmates by pushing, shoving, or yelling, whereas girls would want to talk it out.

Among other possible explanations, they believe this reflects differing physical maturation patterns between boys and girls. Such patterns put girls ahead of boys in terms of language skills; boys are more motor skills oriented at that stage. Even when boys grow up to be men, and girls women, this difference is still evident, though to a lesser degree. That fact is evident to any observer.

A study described in *Scientific American* told of research done to track the effect that varying levels of estrogen (the predominant female hormone) have on female performance abilities.[3] They were investigating whether the different hormonal mix that males and females undeniably carry could be the basis for gender differences. The researchers found that when the women's estrogen level was at its highest (such as during ovulation during the monthly cycle), they performed significantly higher on verbal tests than during the rest of the month. Additionally, they performed most poorly on the spatial tests (tests on which men usually excel) when their estrogen levels were high.

What are the significance of these findings? Put simply, when the maximum female factors are present (for example, high estrogen levels), females perform better on the classically female-dominant tasks (verbal and fine motor skills). Conversely, when estrogen levels are lower, females' test scores on traditionally male-dominated skills (for example, spatial tasks) are higher, more in the range of male test scores.

EMOTIONAL DIFFERENCES

We have also noticed a difference in how males and females handle hurt feelings and other interpersonal conflicts. Boys tend to blow up quickly when angry, then cool down quickly, much like a summertime cloudburst. A girl's response to hurt, on the other hand, more closely resembles a long, sustained winter drizzle. Girls tend to remember for a long time how someone wronged them or hurt them. They can remember every word, every bit of body language at the time of the infraction, every detail of the social setting in which it happened.

When I (Suzette) taught junior high and high school I was amazed at how differently the guys and girls handled anger. If one of the girls got mad over a test score or project grade, she might stay angry for two days. Most girls tend to pout and process longer than boys do. The boys, on the other hand, seemed to recover as soon as they were on to something else, like a discussion of the upcoming basketball game.

Since relationships are very important to girls—and since their brains are wired differently from boys'—they tend to have the memory of an elephant when it comes to others' emotional "crimes." In his book *Tender Warriors*, Stu Weber tells the story of a Swiss psychologist who spent his entire professional life studying the psychology of women, only to blurt out in a moment of frustration, "What is it they want anyway!"[4] As parents, we need to keep that in mind when we want to communicate with our daughters after they've been hurt by us.

DIFFERENT DOESN'T MEAN BETTER OR WORSE

Some people get highly upset whenever male/female differences are discussed. We think that is usually due to a misunderstanding of what is meant by different. Some think this term necessarily implies that one gender is better than the other, but that is not the meaning of different. In the beginning, God created us as different genders on purpose (Genesis 1:27), with oneness in a marriage relationship as one of His primary purposes in bestowing such diversity. It is beautiful to see how in a marriage relationship—or in a family setting—the strengths and weaknesses of each sex can complement each other. That's something to celebrate!

During youth we need to be nurtured in male- and

female-appropriate ways so we can grow up to be the best individuals we can become. Research on the differences between the sexes will probably continue for many years, but there have been solid, statistically valid studies done on certain aspects of the male/female puzzle, and it's certainly legitimate to examine them.

Don't cage in your children according to their sex, though. While understanding some common differences between the genders is helpful in parenting, don't fall into the trap of stereotyping your children by whether they came home wrapped in a blue or pink blanket. There are few "blanket" statements that we can make concerning gender differences. Much of what constitutes male and female behavior and roles is largely a product of our unique cultural setting.

◎

In the next two chapters we'll explore issues of communication, both the verbal and nonverbal aspects. Believe it or not, much more is communicated to our kids in the nonverbal realm than in the verbal. If your family seems to be lacking in the communication process (and whose isn't?), you may be amazed to find out what kind of things are being communicated without words.

THINKING IT OVER

1. What are some gender-based characteristics you have noticed while attending an athletic event? Keep this question in mind the next time you attend a competition.
2. List and discuss conversational differences between the sexes. What significance do you find in these differences?
3. What can you do better to develop your communication skills, especially with regard to relating best to the males and females in your family?

4. What was the most significant thing you learned from this chapter concerning male/female differences? How can you apply this to your relationship with your spouse and/or opposite-sex children?

Notes

1. Norman Geschwind, "Proceedings of the National Academy of Sciences," USA TODAY '79, 1982, pp. 50, 97-100.
2. Janice T. Gibson, "Are Boys and Girls Really So Different?" *Parents* (September 1990): 157.
3. "Profile: Viva La Difference—Doreen Kimura Plumbs Male and Female Brains," *Scientific American* (October 1990): 42.
4. Stu Weber, *Tender Warriors* (Portland, OR: Multnomah, 1993), p. 120.

CHAPTER TEN

The Power of
Nonverbal Communication

MANNERS HAVE ALWAYS BEEN AT THE TOP OF MY (SUZETTE'S) LIST of important things for kids to learn. With my own kids I tried to stress that having good manners was a form of honoring others. Waiting for everyone to be served at the dinner table and putting a napkin in your lap should be automatic procedure as far as I'm concerned. I started teaching this when the kids were very young.

Jim, however, never understood why anyone would want a messy napkin in his lap, so he started secretly slipping it under the tablecloth. He thought he was being entertaining and sneaky. It worked, until I caught the kids with their napkins stuffed under the tablecloth. "Where did you learn to do that?" I demanded. Three pairs of eyes stared in Jim's direction. I looked at Jim in disbelief. "Nice example!" He was caught red-handed.

Modeling is never an option for parents; it's a fact. Our kids are watching our behavior and are soaking it up like sponges. We are models—for good or for bad.

IT'S WHAT YOU DON'T SAY THAT COUNTS

In the next chapter we'll talk about verbal communication, but first we'll discover how nonverbal messages communicate our values and beliefs more strongly than our actual words do.

For instance, I can tell our dog, with my lips, "Sally, you are the ugliest excuse for a flea-bitten, tick-infected, worm-ridden, runny-eyed mutt I've ever seen." But if I say that with a big smile and pleasant tone while gently petting her,

Sally will wag her tail with glee because I've communicated something entirely contrary to the meaning of my words.

And it works just as well in reverse. I can tell Sally how much I love her, but if I do it with a scowl while shaking a stick at her, I communicate anger and hatred rather than affection.

Communication with humans works the same way. Researchers tell us that less than 10 percent of human communication is with actual words. Fully one-third is communicated by tone of voice and more than half by body language.

Gary Smalley and John Trent tell the story of a wife who was frustrated with her husband's angry and dishonoring body language. Inspired by the hidden camera shows on TV, she mounted a small camcorder on a bookshelf and turned it on as soon as she heard her husband's car pull in the driveway at the end of the day. During the evening she brought up her concern about her husband's hostile body language. As he angrily denied such behavior, she revealed the camera and put the tape in the VCR. Her husband was stunned as he watched how many times he had rolled his eyes back, crossed his arms, and refused to make eye contact with his wife. All he could say was, "Is that really me? Do I really look that way?"[1] A family version of "Candid Camera" might be an education for us all.

We wonder if God had the power of nonverbal communication in mind when He commanded the Israelites: "Love the LORD your God with all your heart and with all your soul and with all your strength. These commandments that I give you today are to be upon your hearts. Impress them on your children. Talk about them when you sit at home and when you walk along the road, when you lie down and when you get up" (Deuteronomy 6:5-7).

Notice that the word "talk" is used only once. We are not told to love God with our mouth but with our heart, soul, and strength. God's intention is that our actions clearly reflect that love and be a natural part of every moment of our day. St. Francis of Assisi once stated it well: "Proclaim Christ in everything you do. If necessary, use words."

TRANSFERING VALUES AND BELIEFS

In this way, values and beliefs are more "caught" than "taught." A friend of ours, Jim Watkins, illustrates parenting with the following story. He and his five-year-old son, Paul, decided one weekend to repaint Paul's bike. They spent hours sanding down chipped areas on the fenders and cleaning the chrome sprockets and handlebars. All the while, Paul was getting more and more impatient. "Come on, Dad. When are we going to paint it?"

Finally by Saturday afternoon the time had arrived to paint the bike with gray primer.

"Why do we have to do that?" Paul demanded. "Let's just paint it jet black."

"Well, the primer helps the outside paint to stick on better," Jim tried to explain as he shook the can of spray paint.

"Can I do it, Dad? I'll be careful," Paul said. Jim decided to let his son have a try. Jim thought he had explained the fine art of spray painting to Paul, but once the can of paint was in Paul's hand, the boy aimed it at the back fender and bombarded one small area. Quickly the thick paint began running in little gray rivulets over the edge of the fender.

"Remember, Paul, you have to use real thin coats of paint," Jim warned.

"But it doesn't cover anything that way," countered his son.

"Well, it takes a lot of thin coats. Sometimes the coats aren't even visible. But if you just keep putting on thin coat after thin coat, pretty soon it begins to show." Jim demonstrated as Paul watched in amazement.

Watkins reminds us, "Parenting is like that. If we bombard our children with lectures, the values we want to teach often 'run' — or worse, our children 'run' from us. But it's the many thin coats of advice—backed up by our actions—that begin to slowly build up and produce a high-gloss finish in our children's lives."[2]

We have tried to "spray" several things onto our children through verbal as well as nonverbal communication. Three are at the top of our list.

First is the importance of God. Because our kids are our investment in the future, we view them as our primary disciples. Throughout our lives and after we're gone, we want our kids to remember that their parents loved and honored God above all things. We want them to see this lived out through our actions, attitudes, relationships, and priorities.

Second is the importance of our spouses. Someone has said that one of the most important things a dad can do for his kids is to love their mom. I (Jim) want my tone of voice and body language to demonstrate to my kids that I love and cherish Suzette above all others.

Third is the importance of our children. We must let them know, in word and deed, that they are very high on our priority list. Suzette and I often tell our kids that they are wonderful gifts from God. But because more than half of our daily communication is transmitted through body language, we want everything we *don't* say to communicate their importance to us as well.

Let's go back to the incident when Jill interrupted me by bringing me her spin art project. My smile told her, "It's okay to show me your art even though I'm busy." If I had frowned, rolled my eyes in frustration, crossed my arms, slumped my shoulders, or failed to make eye contact, my actions would have told her silently, but very clearly, "Get lost. I'm busy!" She would have heard loud and clear that she wasn't valuable in my economy.

AFFIRMING OUR CHILDREN'S VALUE

Meaningful touches—pats on the back, friendly punches in the arm, hugs, firm handshakes, and so on—are an important and essential means by which to show others how important they are. Several medical studies have shown that those who receive four or more healthy hugs a day actually have longer life expectancy. In fact, one study revealed that babies who were not held as infants actually died from lack of physical contact—even though all their other physical needs were fulfilled. Make sure your children aren't dying for healthy physical affection.

I (Jim) would sound two cautions as your children become teenagers. First, don't stop hugging them. Many fathers stop hugging their developing daughters just when they need healthy hugging the most. If girls are not getting the minimum daily requirement of meaningful touches at home, they could turn to premature sexual expression in order to get the physical affirmation they need.

Second, be sensitive to your kids' feelings. As children go through puberty, they begin to feel more modest and protective of their bodies. Suzette and I have been diligent at maintaining open, honest communication with our kids about sex and their bodies.

Fortunately, our children have grown up with plenty of hugging and kissing, and they continue to feel free to express healthy physical affection. One spring, I (Jim) went to Travis's football practice at Southwest Missouri State. I made my way under the goal posts where he was practicing kicking. When he saw me we walked toward each other and he initiated a hug at midfield. Not the usual behavior of a typical college athlete whose coaches and teammates were looking on.

There are dozens of other ways parents can communicate how important their children are. For instance, when Jason was six years old, he volunteered to help paint the house. The logical part of me knew he'd get more paint on the driveway and himself than on the house. But I wanted him to feel important, so I forced myself to hand over the paint brush to my Retriever pup.

At dinner—after we had spent an hour cleaning up— Jason proudly announced, "Hey, Mom, I helped Dad paint the house!" Then he turned to me, "Daddy, can I help you paint tomorrow?" Even though I was screaming "no" inside, I wanted Jason to know that I loved him more than I loved perfection. So I said yes.

Another way to communicate value is simply to sit our warm bodies in the audience of a school play or on the bleacher at the soccer field. Our mere presence shouts, "What you're doing at school is important to me! *You* are important to me."

A longtime friend and high school football coach, George Loss, was a real winner when it came to affirming the players on his team. As I worked for George as an inner-city coach, I noticed how he handled interruptions during staff meetings. Instead of telling a player, "Can't you see we're busy?" George stopped whatever we were discussing to hear out his player. No wonder the kids loved George—and knew that he loved them.

SPRAY PAINT AND OTHER ADULTS

Being a single parent as a result of divorce or death is a challenge for many reasons—one being that there is only one adult to provide moral and emotional support for the children. Married couples can be single parents as well because some partners simply refuse to take on their parenting responsibilities and thus remain disengaged—even if they are physically in the home. Perhaps the spouse is addicted to work or alcohol and is not physically or emotionally present when he or she is needed by the children. A serious illness can force the healthy spouse temporarily to become a single parent. And in the case of a remarriage, a child may not accept the new parent, which forces the original parent to assume the single parent role.

If you are a single parent for any of the reasons listed above, you need not handle the full weight of the parenting responsibility yourself. Choose a role model of the same sex as your missing spouse—a man or woman who shares your moral, ethical, and spiritual values. Invite that person to go with you to school activities and events. Ask him or her to spend time with your children. Don't assume that other adults are too busy or too uninterested to help.

Our friend Kathy has raised her two boys, Cody and Jesse, by herself since they were two years and two months old, respectively. She has made sure they've been involved in sports programs and has surrounded them with men who have been good examples. At the same time, she has been a great example to other single moms by going out of her way to make sure her boys have positive male role models.

Even if a child has two parents, positive relationships with other adult role models are important. Kids can use all the love and support they can get, and other relationships can help fill the personality gaps in a family. At least four other couples have helped us raise our own children. Our kids love and respect each of these other adults and enjoy spending time with them. Each of these people has enriched our kids' lives in various ways—with stories, insights, and opinions that have helped mold them into the young adults they are today. Through the years we have been so grateful for a second opinion, especially from an adult with a different personality mix from our own.

SPRAY PAINT AND PEERS

As any parent knows, a child's peers can be powerful role models—for good or for bad. We have made it a point to meet the parents of our children's friends by inviting them to dinner or to ride to out-of-town athletic events with us. We've always encouraged our kids to invite their friends to our home, and we've maintained an "open door/open refrigerator" policy. We want to make life in our home so inviting that the hearts of both our kids and their friends will be attracted to us, rather than to the wrong crowd at school.

For instance, Jason had a friend who loved to hang out at our house. This friend's family was violent, so he was amazed that we didn't shout and throw things at each other. We're not perfect, but we've always worked hard on the quality of our family life. As a result, years later, on each Sunday evening, our kids, their spouses, and their friends show up for dinner. We are thrilled that they still enjoy the atmosphere of our home.

@

Though the importance of nonverbal communication is staggering, the verbal side is crucial, too. In the next chapter we'll explore three secrets to effective verbal interaction with family members. Whether you're blessed with high Otters who talk, talk, talk, or with Retrievers who have to be drawn out verbally, these concepts will help improve this critical area of your family's life.

THINKING IT OVER

1. What are some significant differences between verbal and nonverbal communication? List and/or discuss ways that you have communicated nonverbally in the last couple of days.
2. What would a secret videotape reveal about your use of nonverbals with your family members?
3. Which of your children is most affected by destructive nonverbal communication? Have you experienced her closed spirit when you have used nonverbals to the extreme? In what specific ways can you change your behavior to be more sensitive to her feelings?
4. What areas of communication could you learn that might make you a more effective communicator with those you love?

Notes

1. Gary Smalley and John Trent, *The Two Sides of Love* (Pomona, Calif.: Focus on the Family, 1990), p. 126.
2. Jim Watkins, in a sermon delivered at LaOtto Wesleyan Church, LaOtto, Indiana, on November 11, 1990.

CHAPTER ELEVEN

Talking to the Animals

"YOU WANT TO DO *WHAT*, JASON?" I (JIM) TRIED TO CONTROL THE tone of my voice, but I knew disapproval was coloring my actual words.

"I want to get a Boz haircut." When Jason was in junior high school, Brian Bosworth was a popular pro football player with a haircut that was short on top, shaved on the sides, and long in the back. Such a "do" would have definitely been a head turner in our small town.

As I continued objecting as gently as possible, I didn't pick up on my son's nonverbal messages. His head dropped, his eyes avoided mine, and he dragged himself off to his room. It didn't take me long to realize there must be more to his request than just a new hairstyle. I followed Jason to his room, and after a short discussion, his desire began to make sense. Our Golden Retriever didn't see this as merely a haircut but as a bond between friends. He and his friend Brian had agreed to go to the barber together for their new styles. I had wrongly assumed that my son's desire for a Boz hairstyle meant he was turning anti-establishment. But when I realized that his motive for wanting the haircut was related to a relationship and not to rebellion, I said, "Well, why don't you take some more time to think about it before you actually head for the barber."

As it turned out, Jason decided not to get the haircut. But the incident taught me that I could have seriously damaged all future communication with my son had I not taken the time to hear him out.

This incident points out two important principles. First,

the question our child approaches us with is often not the real issue. For Jason, the haircut was only an indication of a deeper question: "Can I do something with a friend that will deepen our relationship?" Second, many times our children really do want to communicate with us but are afraid of our disapproval. My initial tone of voice and disapproving body language almost stopped communication at skin-deep level.

Suzette and I have not always been so compassionate and understanding with our children or with each other. The ability to communicate well is not automatic or inborn; it's a skill learned over time that takes much practice. Through the years, we have used three tools that have greatly helped the communication within our family.

QUICK LISTENING

There's an old story about a young farmer who was struggling to get his mule to move. He had coaxed it with a carrot and had tried pulling and pushing, but the mule sat stubbornly in the middle of the road.

Finally an old farmer pulled up alongside with his mule and cart. The young farmer explained that he needed to get the load of hay to market, but midway to town the mule had suddenly stopped in its tracks and wouldn't budge.

The old farmer casually walked to the back of his wagon, pulled out a six-foot-long two-by-four, and clobbered the young farmer's mule right between the eyes. The mule leaped forward like lightning—and didn't stop till it reached town.

"First, son," the old farmer advised, "you've got to get the mule's attention."

"Quick listening" is the two-by-four between our eyes that gets our attention so we can listen effectively to our children.

One day I (Jim) was hit between the eyes. Travis kept coming downstairs to the office asking me questions. I would grunt a few "uh huhs," and he would run back up to his room. Finally, after about an hour, Travis came storming downstairs, saying, "It's all your fault, Dad! I don't think you were even listening to me."

"Uh huh."

"Dad!"

"What?" I look up. Travis finally had my attention.

"You weren't listening to me when I was asking you questions. And now look what I've done." I followed Travis as he hurried up to his room. "See!"

There in his bedroom was a full-size basketball goal, board, and pole.

"I put it together like you said, and now I can't get it outside!"

Had I really said "uh huh" to putting together a full-size, regulation basketball goal in his bedroom? If I had just spent thirty seconds really listening to what Travis had asked an hour before, I wouldn't have had to spend thirty minutes helping him get this beast out of his room.

The instructions for this communication tool are in James 1:19. We are to be quick to listen (quick listening), slow to speak (focused on the speaker with no preconceived notions), and (therefore we will be) slow to anger. The secret to quick listening is to give the child your full attention as you watch for both verbal and nonverbal messages. That means no distractions: Turn off the TV, put down the newspaper, swing around from your desk to face him, or hold him on your lap so he knows you're listening—not just with your ears but with your whole body.

Jill's best time to unload was usually at bedtime. We didn't stand by her bed (which would have communicated that we were in a hurry), but rather we either knelt by her bed or sat beside her. That way our body language communicated, *You're the most important person in the world right now.*

One night by Jill's bedside, I (Suzette) asked her, "What happened in school today, Jill?" Her silence (nonverbal message) screamed that something went wrong. "Did something happen today that upset you?"

"Well," Jill stammered, "there were some kids making fun of me because I have to go to the remedial reading lab."

"How did that make you feel?" her dad asked.

Jill paused. She was uncomfortable expressing that feeling. So I prompted, "Are you saying that those kids made you feel like you aren't smart?" Part of quick listening is articulating or repeating to your child what you think you heard her say. If you have it wrong, she'll let you know, and you can try again.

Somberly, Jill's little head bobbed up and down. I wanted to get to a solution, so I gently asked, "Do you have any ideas about what we can do about it?"

Another painful pause. Then she suggested, "Well, maybe we could go to the library more often."

I made a quick decision and said to her, "I have an appointment tomorrow, but I can cancel it so we can go to the library together."

"All right, Mom!" she smiled. She hugged me and snuggled under the covers. The whole conversation took only a very few minutes, yet because I gave her my total attention she was completely satisfied.

I'm not advocating being a one-minute parent. Kids need quantity as well as quality in their relationship with you. But quick listening is one way to open the lines of communication—no matter how busy you become.

One family we know tells about the time their two sons came home from spending the weekend at another family's home. The visit went well in general, but the oldest son,

Jimmy, said to his mother, "Mom, I'm glad we talk a lot in our family."

The mother, a bit puzzled by such a statement out of the blue, wondered what was behind it. "What do you mean, Jimmy? Didn't they allow you to talk during the weekend?"

"Oh, sure, we could talk. But what I meant was that sometimes when the parents were angry with us, they would just glare at us with a hateful look. And I wouldn't know why they were doing it. It made me scared and confused." Apparently one time Jimmy's little brother, Ben, who was an Otter, wasn't getting in the car fast enough for the dad who was a Beaver. He was probably running around the car three times before getting in, just for the fun of it. So instead of simply telling Ben, "Please get in the car now," the man glared at him and Jimmy.

"Mom, I'm glad that in our family when we're upset with another person, we just say so. That way we know where we stand and don't have to worry so much."

We can't overemphasize the importance of talking out feelings in the family setting. Friction is a natural thing in families and need not be destructive if it's handled in a straightforward and honest manner. Unexplained nonverbals such as sizzling glares don't help at all.

EMOTIONAL BAROMETERS

Suzette is the most balanced person I (Jim) know, but the Lion in her wants to get to the point.

Earlier in our marriage, there were times when she would ask me, "What's wrong?" she expected a concise answer. But because I'm an Otter/Retriever, my answers tended to wander and dwell mostly on how I was feeling about the issue. This would frustrate her until "Just give me a straight answer!" would bubble out. As we've come to understand our personality differences through the years, Suzette has changed her approach with both me and our children.

We both have learned to ask our kids, "On a scale of one to ten, how do you feel about such and such?" For instance, once I needed to know how Travis felt about staying home with Jill while Suzette and I went to one of Jason's ball games. An eight or ten would tell us, "Yeah, that would be great!" Something under four would mean, "That's really the last thing I'd like to do." Regardless of the decision we made about the babysitting arrangement, using the emotional barometer tool would help us gather immediate and accurate information about our son's feelings, which would help us communicate with him better.

Using the emotional barometer is good for simple checks, but for more complex issues and feelings we use emotional word pictures.

EMOTIONAL WORD PICTURES[1]

Because word pictures depict what words cannot communicate, they have become an integral part of our family communication. When Suzette and I had been married for about twelve years, I really needed a way to express to her how I felt when I walked in the door and was confronted with a list of family responsibilities I had neglected. I had never told her my true feelings.

Finally one night, after suspending three students, severely reprimanding one teacher, and losing a football game, I was met at the door with, "Why can't you help around the house? Why don't you spend time with the kids? All you do is hide away in the den watching films of next week's football opponents."

I was also met at the door by our black Labrador, her tail

wagging, showing how glad she was to see me. At that moment I thought of the ideal word picture. I practiced explaining it a few times with a close friend from school so I would get it right when I talked with my wife. Then that evening when the kids were asleep and Suzette and I were in bed, I pulled her close to me.

"Honey, do you remember going coon hunting with your granddaddy?" Suzette loved her grandfather, so she was instantly on-line with me as she fondly remembered those days.

"Remember how he told us that sometimes one of the coon dogs would get lost? Grandaddy would leave a blanket with his scent on the ground. The next morning the exhausted hound, who was bruised and bloodied from finding its way back through the underbrush, would be lying on the blanket, eagerly awaiting the joyful reunion with his master."

Suzette snuggled closer as I continued.

"But what if your granddaddy, instead of hugging and comforting the dog, took off his belt and beat him for getting lost. 'Bad dog!' he would shout."

Suzette stiffened in my arms at the picture of such cruelty. I took a deep breath before going on.

"Suzette, that's how I feel when I come home from a day of giving and giving and giving, and you beat me at the door with, 'Why didn't you do this and that?'"

There was a long, heavy silence. "Oh, Jim," she said, "I had no idea that's how you felt."

Although I didn't know how powerful this word picture would be, the feelings it captured brought to the surface all the emotions we'd been repressing, and that really surprised us both. After nearly two hours of tears and soul searching, we reached a deeper level of mutual understanding. It was painful, but working through such a significant problem brought us together in a way that nothing else could.

A few weeks later, I was on the receiving end of another powerful word picture. The kids were at a babysitter's house, and Suzette and I were enjoying an evening at our favorite frozen yogurt shop.

"Remember those chocolate-covered strawberries you enjoy during the summer?" Suzette asked.

Remember? I could taste them! I used to stand in long lines during tourist season in Branson for those wonderful chocolate-covered strawberries.

Suzette continued. "Imagine that The Fudge Shop just made their last batch of the season."

"You bet I can," I replied enthusiastically.

"Well, imagine, Jim, that you're the last person in line waiting to make your final purchase of the season. You watch intently as each person checks out at the cash register. Your mouth is watering so badly that you have to keep swallowing to avoid drooling. Finally, you step up to the counter in eager anticipation, only to hear the clerk announce they just sold their last strawberry. How would that make you feel?"

"I'd feel cheated and totally frustrated," I quickly answered.

Now it was Suzette's turn to take a deep breath and knock the wind out of me. "That's how I feel, Jim. Every night when you come home, I'm the last person in that long, long line."

I stared in disbelief at my empty yogurt dish. "I don't understand."

"Every day it's as if you're that clerk," she began. "You give and give and give to everyone at school, but when you finally come home to the kids and me you're 'all sold out.' There's nothing left for us. You escape with the newspaper or TV, and we feel cheated and frustrated because you don't have anything left to give us."

Just as Suzette had no idea for twelve years how I'd felt

when I came home from work, I'd had no idea how she'd felt. I didn't quit my job, but I did start looking at my day in a radically different way. I had been lulled into the world's mold of the conquering male who works at the office, then comes home to relax with his slippers and the evening paper. I began to rearrange my priorities at the office. I delegated more work to others. I also began to realign my spiritual priorities. After what seemed to be a season of prayer, I sensed the power to help me get through a stressful day and still have strength to be with and enjoy my family.

One practical thing I did was cancel the newspaper subscription and spend the time finding out my family's daily news. And I found myself more motivated to help Suzette around the house. As a result I became a better model of how a man should love his wife and family. I began to see tense situations not as problems to drain me but rather as trials that could make me a better person—and a better husband and father.

Suzette and I have used this same word picture method with our children. For instance, one day Jason—who was on the verge of driver's education—said, "I feel like a '57 Chevy." So I played along and asked, "What condition is the car in? Does it have bright, shiny paint and a mint-condition interior? Or is the paint scratched up and are the taillights kicked out?"

"Well, I feel like I've been rear-ended," Jason answered. "I feel like all weekend long all I've gotten from you is negative feedback. You've been kicking my tail all weekend, and I feel pretty emotionally banged up."

Again I felt I'd been broadsided. I guess I'd been kidding Jason a lot that weekend. What I thought was good-natured humor had felt like cruel put-downs to my son. Once I was made aware of that, we were able to work through our misunderstanding.

Consider using something your child really enjoys in your word picture. If he's taking music lessons ask, "What kind of music do you feel like today? Rock, jazz, gospel, rap, or a funeral dirge?" If she loves stuffed animals ask, "Which one of your animals do you feel most like?" Then ask why. You'll discover that she feels like the droopy-eyed puppy because she's sad about something that happened at school. Or she may pick a funny clown because that's how she feels at the moment.

Some readers may think emotional word pictures are simply a tool to manipulate others—find a person's most sensitive nerve, open it up, and pour acid on it. Please understand, the purpose is not to scald the other person but to let him see something important in the relationship. The goal of a word picture is to get the other person to feel your genuine feelings so you can communicate more effectively.

◉

We've covered a lot of information so far. Understanding personality types and basic parenting skills is extremely helpful in enhancing family life, but it's only a good foundation. There comes a time in implementing these concepts when you have to blend that understanding together with healthy portions of respect, love, and family loyalty. Our last chapter covers these crucial ingredients.

THINKING IT OVER

1. Why does "just saying no" to your child elicit a chorus of "Why?" How does a child's response differ according to his or her personality type?
2. How can you keep lines of communication open with your teenager when he tells you something that shocks you?

3. What conditions exist in your home (or heart) that hinder you from "quick listening"? Try this technique and share its benefits with a friend or fellow parent this week.

4. When is the best time for your child to communicate to you how his or her day went? Have you been taking advantage of this time in an effective way?

5. What are some of your children's favorite toys, games, cars, and so on? With this in mind, make up an emotional word picture that would motivate them to help around the house, help settle a conflict, or let them know how you feel about them. Try it out on the children, then discuss the results with your spouse or a friend.

Notes

1. This concept was popularized by John Trent and Gary Smalley in *The Language of Love* (Pomona, Calif.: Focus on the Family, 1988). If you would like to know more about emotional word pictures, we suggest you read that book.

CHAPTER TWELVE

From the Jungle to the Game Preserve

(JIM) HAD BLOWN IT WITH JASON. BUT I WASN'T READY TO ADMIT it—at least not yet.

We both avoided eye contact as we drove along in silence—until we were about three or four minutes from school where I was to drop him off. It was now or never.

"Jason, I was wrong. I shouldn't have gotten all over your case when you were running late for school. Maybe having you get up earlier than Travis is the solution, but we can talk about that later. It's just that I don't want you to carry this inside the school doors with you today, so I'm admitting that I was wrong. Will you please forgive me?"

"Yeah, Dad, I will," Jason said, as our eyes finally connected.

I gratefully replied, "I know we don't have time to talk about it right now, but tonight we'll talk it over."

"That'd be great, Dad," Jason replied with a big smile. I watched him bound off toward the school's entrance.

I was glad our relationship had been restored before I turned my son out into that deep, dark jungle. Now he could go through the day looking forward to getting back to the Brawner game preserve, rather than trying to find comfort and acceptance in a hostile world.

Some of the tragic trends we see everywhere today could be avoided if parents would make their home a loving refuge where children could receive the emotional strength and affirmation they need to make it through the tough days. A song recorded by country singer Ronnie Milsap extols a man's love for his wife, especially regarding this idea of refuge:

She keeps the home fires burning
While I'm out earning a living in a world
that's known for its pouring rain.

She keeps the home fires burning.
And it's her warm loving
that keeps me returning again . . . and again.[1]

Our world is often full of pouring rain, and the hotter we stoke the home fires, the more our family members are going to be attracted to and draw their support from home's hearth. If we want our kids to seek shelter from the jungle in our family preserve, we need to make our home a safe, respectful, loving environment.

CULTIVATING MUTUAL RESPECT

A crucial part of making your home a place your kids will want to be is to cultivate an environment where it is safe to express oneself, where each member of the family can be respectfully heard. One way we have tried to create this safety in our home is through family goal-setting meetings. We didn't always schedule them; they were sometimes spontaneous—held on our king-sized bed or around the dinner table. They were called whenever we needed to plan a family vacation or party, settle a conflict, or develop a new family policy.

For example, when we were preparing to choose a second family car that the kids would use, we got the whole family involved. At all our family meetings we used the acrostic G-O-A-L-S as a kind of agenda. The first stage is G for "gather." We gather as many ideas as possible. (At this stage it's all green-light thinking. No idea is criticized as we talk.) Sometimes we write down our ideas on three-by-five cards; other times we just call them out and write them down on an erasable markerboard.

"I think you should get a customized van."

"No, a Lambourghini!"

"I want a minivan."

"I want a Porsche!"

"How about a Jeep to go camping with?"

"Or maybe a pickup with a camper."

Everyone — no matter how young — has a chance to express his or her thoughts and desires. Otters have the most fun with this stage, so tap into their creativity. Lions, however, are wanting to move on to the bottom line, so try to hold them back if necessary to complete the whole decision-making process.

The next step is O for "organize." We begin to categorize our ideas. This is where the Beavers can use their gifts to the fullest since they are masters of organization.

"Let's see, these ideas break down into categories of vans, Jeeps, and sports cars."

Notice that in these first two stages, no one is allowed to say, "That's a dumb idea."

Only at the third stage, A, should the family begin to "analyze" how practical the ideas are. The power of reasoning takes over in this phase. The Golden Retriever is especially good here because he takes each person into consideration.

"I don't think a sports car or a pickup truck would work for a family of five." Notice that the idea is what is being analyzed, not the person who came up with the idea.

L is for "limit." Together, the family crosses off ideas that are beyond their financial or time resources. When we went through this process, the prices ranged between $150 and $19,000. Needless to say, the Lambourghini was crossed off the list. Lions love the bottom-line mentality of this limiting phase.

For decisions that affect the whole family, you'll also need to cross off ideas that someone in the family just can't live with.

"I would be embarrassed to go to school in a pickup truck with a camper," Jason said. (Jason, as a married man, has a pickup with a camper top. Ironic!)

Going through this whole process as a family helps each personality see the importance of each step. Otters tend to be great idea people but often lack follow-through. Beavers aren't always creative in the gathering stage but shine in the organizing phase. Lions are confident decision-makers when a final choice is required. And Golden Retrievers' desire for harmony keeps the whole process from degenerating into thermonuclear family war.

Finally, after a decision is made, the move is made to S for "start." Unless action is instigated after the discussion, the process is simply dreaming and really not goal setting or decision making. We started looking through newspaper ads, checking out dealerships, and talking to friends and a trusted mechanic.

A GOALS session like this also can be an effective way to handle major discipline issues or resolve conflicts. Our friends, Rod and Vicki, have used this tool with their two sons, Justin and Ryan.

"We seem to have a conflict over who watches what programs on TV," Rod told the boys. "Let's do some 'green-light thinking' and see if we can come up with some solutions."

"You and Mom could buy us each a TV for our own rooms," Justin offered eagerly. Rod had to restrain himself from throwing up a barricade at that suggestion.

"Maybe we could watch some shows live while video-taping a show that somebody else wants to watch," Ryan suggested.

"Or we could all make a list of our three favorite programs

and then rotate through them so everyone gets to watch his very favorites," Vicki said. (Can you guess what kind of personality type would make that suggestion?)

"How about the one who does the dishes that night gets first pick of what shows we watch?" (This child wants to have credit where credit is due!)

After Gathering ideas, this family Organized them, Analyzed them for practicality, Limited them (the family budget just didn't allow three TVs), and then they Started in. The decision was made that each family member would make a list of his favorite shows. Then if there were two shows on at the same time, the family would take turns watching one show while taping the other. Everyone got to watch their preferred shows, and family harmony was restored.

I (Jim) even used the G-O-A-L-S system when beginning plans to build our house. I handed out a piece of paper to each family member and said, "Okay, everyone, pretend this paper is a thirty-by-forty-foot box with two floors. What are we going to put in it?" Jason and Travis wanted a weight and exercise room. Jill wanted a hot tub and a huge closet in her bedroom. Suzette wanted each part of the house to be open so we could communicate wherever we happened to be. We didn't get everything we wanted, but it was a time of bonding as we tackled the job of designing our house and then subcontracting out the work. Today it's "our" house, which highlights another of our goals as parents: building family loyalty.

BUILDING FAMILY LOYALTY

Our kids have always loved having their friends over to their house. I'm sure some of the reason for that is they have ownership in its design. But ownership also includes the rules and regulations of a home. I (Jim) was made aware of that by my high school football coach. He established a discipline committee of three players who decided whether someone who broke training rules would just run laps or be kicked off the team. He wanted the players to own our disciplinary policy.

The coach was a believer in the K-I-S-S principle (Keep It Simple, Silly). He never resorted to anything fancy in terms of game strategy, but he instilled in us an incredible loyalty to the team. We owned our team, our discipline, and our training. As a result, we went from a 0-win, 12-loss season to one game short of a state championship one year later. And our coach succeeded, too. He has been an assistant coach for several National Football League teams.

If your family team feels they have had a say in the outing, discipline, or conflict resolution at hand, they will be more likely to support it. Plus, they'll grow personally in the process.

LOVE CURES ALL

A study several years ago set out to determine if lenient or restrictive parents produced the healthiest kids. Researchers examined families of military men, where all was spit-and-polish. Then they examined very laissez-faire families, where there was hardly any structure at all. What they discovered is that those kinds of environmental variables made no significant difference. Kids turned out great in both environments as long as a key element was in place: love and acceptance. High-quality relationships are the key to family success.

Sometimes the tendency after reading a book on personality types is to think, *Well, I'm just a Lion, so I really can't help but growl and snarl at the kids.* Don't give up so easily! Don't think you can't change and improve. And don't give up on your children, even if they're nearly grown.

Over the years, our Lion Travis has become more sensitive and has developed some wonderful Golden Retriever qualities. And this Otter dad has even developed some Beaver traits, especially while working on this book. Double-strength Otter Jill has learned some effective organizational skills. Jason has gotten much better at doing what is especially hard for a Retriever to do—saying no. And Lionish Suzette has learned to temper her get-to-the-point approach. The secret is to keep cultivating the areas that are weak or lacking, while continually working on open and loving relationships.

None of us can be a perfect parent, and the concepts in this book are certainly not meant to condemn anyone. They're meant to help you understand yourself and the makeup of your kids. Sometimes that's half the battle. And if you think you've blown it in parenting, welcome to the club. The task of raising kids is awesome and can feel overwhelming, but keep two things in mind:

1. Love covers a multitude of sins.
2. Never give up.

In other words, remember that if you spread enough love around your home, your mistakes will pale in the light of your love. The apostle John wrote, "Perfect love drives out fear" (1 John 4:18). Regardless of how many minor mistakes you make, if you love your kids enough, they'll turn out much better than if you stop trying to connect with them.

Bill Cosby, who became one of America's best-known dads on the TV show, "The Cosby Show," makes some lighthearted comments in his best-selling book, *Fatherhood*, that should encourage all parents:

> It is no profound revelation to say that fathering has changed greatly from the days when my own father

used me for batting practice. However, the baffling behavior of children is exactly the same today as it was when Joseph's brothers peddled him to the Egyptians. And in the face of such constantly baffling behavior, many men have wondered: Just what is a father's role today . . . ?

The answer, of course, is that no matter how hopeless or copeless a father may be, his role is simply to be there, sharing all the chores with his wife. Let her have the babies; but after that, try to share every job around. Any man today who returns from work, sinks into a chair, and calls for his pipe is a man with an appetite for danger. Actually, changing a diaper takes much less time than waxing a car. A car doesn't spit on your pants, of course, but a baby's book value is considerably higher.

If the new American father feels bewildered and even defeated, let him take comfort from the fact that whatever he does in any fathering situation has a fifty percent chance of being right. Having five children has taught me a truth as cosmic as any that you can find on a mountain in Tibet: There are no absolutes in raising children. In any stressful situation, fathering is always a roll of the dice. The game may be messy, but I have never found one with more rewards and joys.

You know the only people who are always sure about the proper way to raise children? Those who've never had any.[2]

As we've seen, good parenting involves listening intently to our children, making them a priority in our lives, and valuing their unique personality makeup. It means trashing the one-size-fits-all parenting method and adapting our approach to each unique child. It means continually strengthening our partnership with God as we guide and love our children. We need all the help we can get!

If we lean on Him and hang in there, trying each day to be the best parents we can be, all the while flavoring our relationships with generous amounts of love, we're going to have the success we desire. May God help us all to be more like Him as we raise a generation of healthy, happy kids who can handle anything this world throws their way.

THINKING IT OVER

1. What are the advantages of including everyone in your family in the decision-making process? What decision does your family currently face that could benefit from using the G-O-A-L-S process?
2. Do your family members regularly seek shelter in the game preserve you call home? Why or why not?
3. How does your family measure up in terms of the crucial elements of family harmony: respect, loyalty, and love? Which area do you as a parent most need to work on?
4. The saying goes, "Feed your faith, and doubt will starve to death." What can you do to strengthen your own faith (and your children's faith) so you can stand firm against the pressures of the world?

Notes

1. Mike Reid, Don Pfrimmer, Dennis Morgan, "She Keeps the Home Fires Burning." Copyright 1985 by Lodge Hall Music, Inc., c/o MBG Songs, Inc., Collins Court Music, Inc., and Tom Collins Music, Inc. All rights reserved. Used by permission.
2. Bill Cosby, *Fatherhood* (New York: Berkeley, 1986), pp. 60-61.

Appendix

OTHER PERSONALITY TYPING SYSTEMS

THE T-JTA

The Taylor-Johnson Temperament Analysis test contains 180 statements that respondents answer either "decidedly so," "undecided," or "decidedly not."

Using a rather complicated scoring procedure, the results are graphed on a continuum between composed and nervous, light-hearted and depressive, active-social and quiet, expressive-responsive and inhibited, sympathetic and indifferent, objective and subjective, dominant and submissive, tolerant and hostile, as well as self-disciplined and impulsive.

BIRTH ORDER

Kevin Leman's best-selling book *The Birth Order Book* attempts to explain why you are the way you are by dividing people into three broad groups: firstborns, second- (or middle-) borns, and last-borns. This psychologist believes that birth order affects our personality, whom we marry, our children, our occupational choice, and even how we relate to God.

Firstborns, according to Dr. Leman, tend to be aggressive, conscientious, overorganized perfectionists. They often bite off more than they can chew because they want to please other people.

Second- or middle-borns seem to have more people-oriented social skills. The stereotype of the overlooked and underappreciated middle child tends to have some validity, according to Dr. Leman. They are often the peacemakers and negotiators in the family.

The last-borns tend to be coddled, so their messy, "somebody will bail me out," self-centered bent is often reinforced. They are usually people-persons, with a gift to be funny, charming, and persuasive.

Like all personality researchers, Dr. Leman stresses that these categories only reflect general tendencies.

THE MMPI

The Minnesota Multiphasic Personality Inventory (MMPI) is a rather technical test, that is typically used by psychiatrists and psychologists in clinical situations where moderate-to-extreme dysfunction is present. It features 566 true/false questions that attempt to predict how a certain person will act or react in a given situation. The test is viewed as quite reliable in revealing how paranoid, depressed, manic, or anxious a person might be. It even includes a "validity scale" intended to measure if a person is lying or answering questions randomly. It is not, however, a simple test to be used and/or understood by laypeople.

THE MYERS-BRIGGS PERSONALITY TYPE INDICATOR

This system, which is fairly easily understood and commonly used by both laypeople and professionals in understanding personality style, divides people into four ways of interacting with others and their environment.[1] The four scales place a person's style somewhere along a continuum: introvert/ extrovert, sensing/intuitive, thinking/feeling, judging/perceiving.

The first scale describes where you relate best. Extroverts

are not necessarily the life of the party or the classic used-car salesmen. Extroverts draw their mental and emotional energy from interacting with the outside world of people or things. Introverts are not always wallflowers or accountants. Introverts would rather spend time in their inner world of ideas and concepts. Extroverts generate the best ideas by brainstorming with others. Introverts prefer to go off by themselves and stare into space, yet they still generate great ideas.

The second scale, Sensing and Intuitive, describes how you gather information. The Sensing type enjoys perceiving with his or her five senses. They like things that can be seen, heard, felt, tasted, or smelled. Intuitive types, however, look at possibilities, associations, and symbols. For instance, a Sensing type would see a brilliant red sunset, while an Intuitive type would "see" good weather tomorrow.

The third set of opposites describes how a person makes choices. A Thinking type is not necessarily emotionless, but he or she does want decisions to be "imminently logical." A Feeling type, on the other hand, is not illogical or irrational but makes decisions on the basis of personal values.

The final pair of types are Judging and Perceiving. The Judging type has already skipped over this entire section of the book because he or she is goal-oriented. Perceiving types are still with us because they view decision-making as a process and remain open to new information, insights, and experiences.

Using these four scales it's possible to come up with sixteen different personality types. David Keirsey, a clinical psychologist, has broken these types down to four general temperaments which roughly correspond to our Lion, Otter, Retriever, and Beaver model.[2]

Notes

1. An excellent Christian perspective of the Myers-Briggs is the book *One of a Kind* by LaVonne Neff, (Portland: Multnomah, 1988).
2. Neff, p. 67.

Authors

JIM and SUZETTE BRAWNER are both graduates of the University of Arkansas. They spent several years in education and as directors at Kanakuk Kamp, a Christian sports camp in Branson, Missouri. They currently are working with relationship consultant and author Gary Smalley at Today's Family where Jim is the national seminar director and Suzette is the director of public relations. The Brawners have three children: Jason, who is married to Alison; Travis; and Jill.

PRACTICAL PARENTING HELP

Daughters and Dads

Here's practical help for dads! Filled with letters from adolescent girls to their dads, this book offers guidance to fathers struggling to understand their changing role in their daughter's life.

Daughters and Dads
(Chap & Dee Clark) $11

Parenting with Love and Logic

Need help with your kids? Learn how to parent with love and logic and be amazed at the results!

Parenting with Love and Logic
(Foster Cline & Jim Fay) $18

Unlocking Your Child's Learning Potential

Discover how your child learns best and ways to communicate that information with teachers. You can help your child succeed in both school and life!

Unlocking Your Child's Learning Potential
(Cheri Fuller) $14

Get your copies today at your local bookstore, or call (800) 366-7788 and ask for offer **#2057**.

NAVPRESS
BRINGING TRUTH TO LIFE
www.navpress.org

Prices subject to change without notice.